Gadda Goes to War

Gadda Goes to War

Translational Provocations Around
An Emergency

Presents Fabrizio Gifuni's award-winning drama
L'ingegner Gadda va alla guerra – in the English
translation, with facing Italian

Edited by Federica G. Pedriali

EDINBURGH
University Press

Edinburgh University Press Ltd
22 George Square, Edinburgh EH8 9LF

www.euppublishing.com

Typeset in 10.5/13 Sabon by
Servis Filmsetting Ltd, Stockport, Cheshire,
and printed and bound in Great Britain by
CPI Group (UK) Ltd, Croydon CR0 4YY

A CIP record for this book is available from the British Library

ISBN 978 0 7486 6871 7 (hardback)
ISBN 978 0 7486 6872 4 (paperback)
ISBN 978 0 7486 6873 1 (webready PDF)
ISBN 978 0 7486 6874 8 (epub)

A *Gaddus Scholars* publication

Publication sponsored by the Edinburgh Gadda Projects and Finmeccanica UK.

Contents

Acknowledgments   vi

Abbreviations   viii

Preface, *Fabrizio Gifuni*   ix

Introduction, *Federica G. Pedriali*   1

PART I

Circulation, *Cristina Olivari and Federica G. Pedriali*   7

Translation, *Christopher John Ferguson*   20

Staging, *Giuseppe Episcopo and Federica G. Pedriali*   36

World-making, *Federica G. Pedriali*   46

Resources, *Alberto Godioli*   58

PART II

Gadda Goes to War – or The tragic story of Hamlet Pirobutirro – with facing Italian, *Fabrizio Gifuni*   76

Global glossary, *Alberto Godioli and Federica G. Pedriali*   129

APPENDIX

Gadda, heal thyself, *Federica G. Pedriali*   141

Bibliography   146

Contributors   162

Index   164

Acknowledgments

In this project, agents (people) have supported the original text by Fabrizio Gifuni to achieve its translation via combined (and collective) translational strategies involving an extended number of agents (other people), platforms (such as performance and public engagement initiatives) and complementary outcomes (including scholarly events and their further outputs), and resulting in the *text* feeding back as *texts* (performance, translation, illustration, subtitles, surtitles, scholarship) to its beneficiaries (again but not conclusively, *people*). In the end, the concepts behind the book unfolded also as the third edition of the Edinburgh Gadda Prize, *Gadda è teatro | Scholarship is engagement*, Edinburgh 2012 for short. This allowed the bringing together of a further series of firsts – among them, the first postgraduate summer school *Gaddus Scholars* (under the title *Great irregulars Body irregular*) and the first international Gadda Juniors mobility programme (which resulted in the multimedia installation *Hybridity*), as well as the UK premiere of *L'ingegner Gadda va alla guerra*, Traverse Theatre, 20–22 September 2012. Indeed, very many people – scholars, editors, translators, stage managers, technicians, panel judges, teachers, trainers, prize participants, students, pupils, helpers, fundraisers, sponsors, government and education officials – have made this level of collective effort possible. We would like to thank them for their commitment, support, vision and active participation – with special thanks to Fabrizio Gifuni, Gualtiero Pedriali, Timothy O'Shea, Dorothy Miell, Arnaldo Liberati, Giorgio Pinotti, Paola Italia, Emilio Manzotti, Andrea Silvestri, Corrado Bologna, Gian Mario Anselmi, Niva Lorenzini, Paolo Bartoloni, Federico Bertoni, Giuseppe Bonifacino, Raffaele Donnarumma, Harald Hendrix, Monica Jansen, Stefano Jossa, Davide Messina, Gino Ruozzi, Maria Bortoluzzi, Giovanna Caltagirone, Giulio de Jorio Frisari, Laura Parola, Emanuele Serafini, Tony Crolla, Cesidio Di Ciacca, Luigi Frigerio,

Guido Pegna, Paolo Relli, Laura Pasetti, Ann Marie Di Mambro, Nicola McCartney, David Williams, Jonathan Gibbs, Lefke Kerr, Astrid Jaeckel, Lucinda Byatt, Silvana Vitale, James Clayton Jones, Emma Lacroix, Giuseppe Episcopo, Carlo Pirozzi, Susanna Grazzini, Giulia Trentacosti, Serena Mariani, the students of the Gadda Honours course class 2013, the families hosting the Italian Gadda Juniors, Evan Thomas and the Stills Gallery, Gwen Orr and the staff at the Traverse Theatre, Jackie Jones and the (exceptionally patient) editors at Edinburgh University Press.

The text and the video recording of *L'ingegner Gadda va alla guerra* are reproduced by kind permission of Fabrizio Gifuni, Fondazione Solares delle Arti, Parma, and Minimum Fax, Rome. The extracts from *Giornale di guerra e di prigionia*, *Eros e Priapo* and *La cognizione del dolore* are reprinted by kind permission of Arnaldo Liberati and the Gadda Estate, Garzanti Libri, Milan, and Adelphi Edizioni, Milan.

Abbreviations

Unless otherwise indicated, Gadda's works are referenced giving: (a) title and date of publication; (b) abbreviated volume title (full listing in the Bibliography); and (c) present location in the five-volume edition, plus Indices, of the Collected Works – *Opere*, edited by Dante Isella (Milan: Garzanti, 1988–93) – with the following abbreviations:

RR I   *Romanzi e racconti*, Vol. I, edited by R. Rodondi, G. Lucchini and E. Manzotti, Milan: Garzanti, 1988.

RR II   *Romanzi e racconti*, Vol. II, edited by G. Pinotti, D. Isella and R. Rodondi, Milan: Garzanti, 1989.

SGF I   *Saggi giornali favole e altri scritti*, Vol. I, edited by L. Orlando, C. Martignoni and D. Isella, Milan: Garzanti, 1991.

SGF II   *Saggi giornali favole e altri scritti*, Vol. II, edited by C. Vela, G. Gaspari, G. Pinotti, F. Gavazzeni, D. Isella and M. A. Terzoli, Milan: Garzanti, 1992.

SVP   *Scritti vari e postumi*, edited by A. Silvestri, C. Vela, D. Isella, P. Italia and G. Pinotti, Milan: Garzanti, 1993.

BI   *Bibliografia e indici*, edited by D. Isella, G. Lucchini and L. Orlando, Milan: Garzanti, 1993.

Other abbreviations

EJGS   *The Edinburgh Journal of Gadda Studies* – http://www.gadda. ed.ac.uk. Journal founded and directed by Federica G. Pedriali.

Qdi   *I quaderni dell'ingegnere. Testi e studi gaddiani*. Journal founded by Dante Isella and directed by Clelia Martignoni.

Preface: Gadda (Pasolini) and the theatre. A sacred act of knowledge

Fabrizio Gifuni

The text and the video recording of the performance presented in this volume are part of a wider theatrical initiative that has been developing over time. At the heart of the project was the desire to organise a grand account of the transformation of Italy: what we were, what we have become and what we have perhaps always been. In this way, I thought, we might understand how we can have arrived at this point. A map of the chromosomes of Italy and its people, this is what I had in mind, so that we might better orient ourselves in a present which is too often dark, opaque and dangerous.

For this reason, some ten years ago I began a long and enthusiastic journey with Giuseppe Bertolucci, borrowing the words of two among the greatest Italian writers of the twentieth-century, Pier Paolo Pasolini and Carlo Emilio Gadda. I felt that there was a strong connection there, despite the diametrical opposition in terms of education, artistic vision, language and view of history. Through various phases of work, between 2004 and 2010 two performances came to life: 'Na specie de cadavere lunghissimo, from texts by Pasolini and from a poem by Giorgio Somalvico, and L'ingegner Gadda va alla guerra o della tragica istoria di Amleto Pirobutirro, based on texts by Gadda with interpolations from Hamlet.

What has emerged from this double take is a relentless stereoscope of our recent past. Pasolini's civil reflections on the anthropological transformation of an entire country come together, like the tiles of a unique mosaic, with Gadda's notes on the Great War and his psychoanalytical interpretation of fascism. Two very different artistic and philosophical visions thus get interlinked, the qualifiers standardly applied in this case – progressive and conservative – finally giving way to the sheer force of two intellects in continuous movement. A furious love for one's country is what provides the common ground: a love which wins these two writers, on the field of battle as it were, the right to pass judgment on what they are witnessing. It is for this reason, I believe, or more precisely, it is because Gadda and Pasolini tear themselves to pieces through their commitment to their country, that their words have, today, a specific and substantial weight, as if they were loaded with a special form of authority. From the act of self-demolition, from the constant shipwrecking of the self, Gadda and Pasolini derive, in fact, the force of their reasoning as well as of their writing. In this spiritual yet secular exercise resides, I argue, the ethical status of their thinking – for it is not enough to express high-mindedness and agreeable thought. One must earn the respect of others.

Just as was the case for the work on Pasolini, *L'ingegner Gadda va alla guerra* is based on texts which were not originally intended for the stage. My first study dates back to a reading I made at the Museo della Fanteria, Rome, in 2006. The sources that I finally chose to disassemble and reaggregate into a new text, this time destined for the theatre, were *Giornale di guerra e di prigionia* and *Eros e Priapo*, as well as two discarded fragments from Gadda's major novel *La cognizione del dolore*. The first text, the *Giornale di guerra e di prigionia*, is the direct testimony of Gadda's participation in the First World War (Infantry, 5th Alpine Regiment), from 24 May 1915 – the first day of training for Sottotenente Gadda at the stores in Edolo – to the first days of 1919, when the future author of *Quer pasticciaccio brutto de via Merulana* returns home after almost two years of imprisonment in a German war camp. *Eros e Priapo*, written in all likelihood in 1944–5, takes instead the literary form of a libellous pamphlet attacking the erotic psychopathology of the Prime Minister, Benito Mussolini, and the pathological attraction that the Italian people have, periodically, for tyrannical figures affected by what Gadda calls narcissistic delirium. Written in a reinvented sixteenth-century Florentine Italian and subtitled *Da furore a cenere* (*From Fury to Ashes*), the book dissects the erotic ties that unify power with the masses through a dizzying linguistic excursion based on notions taken from psychoanalysis.

Fusing these two texts together is the job of Hamlet, Prince of Denmark, and of Longone, the village of Gadda's childhood and family holidays. Hamlet is a lot more than just a literary passion for our author. Gadda joins himself, one might say, to this character as if to an archetype that profoundly represents his life story. An awareness of one's own intellectual stature within a society and a time that are 'out of joint' is what they primarily share. They also have the same devastating relationship with their mothers, whom they similarly locate in the centre of a lethal web of lies from which they must free themselves. Predisposed to melancholia and excited by infinite neuroses, both in the end are constrained, in order that they might live in the world, to pretend to have a particular form of madness. So if Hamlet ends up taking on the role of Yorick, the ideal court jester of his childhood, Gadda will transform himself into the literary genius we know, disappearing behind a language that is out of the ordinary, indeed *extra-ordinary* – a mad gamble turned into a new way to communicate with the world.

This is why I took to imagining Gadda as a no longer young Hamlet with no father or mother to invoke or curse: more nervous, more choleric, left alone with his ghosts, his language buffeted by flashes of protean genius. Always on the verge of a tragic madness, yet at times also hilariously comical, and rich in method. Yes, rich in method. An Amleto Pirobutirro, in sum, not just Gonzalo Pirobutirro, as in Gadda's novel – even though in the novel too the Hamletian motif was rich. A newer protagonist of *La cognizione del dolore*, shadowing Gadda's greatest story, a further alter ego rewinding the tape of his neuroses, and walking slantways, like a crab, on the table of his memories. The resulting descent into a hell of old wounds that had never healed over, till the original wound appears to have been arrived at, leaves this new character – part Gadda, part Hamlet-Gadda – at the existential lowest point possible, which is also the mine of his immense art. His participation in the Great War, the defeat at Caporetto, his detention in the German prison camps and the death of his younger brother Enrico – all of this will change the writer's life and that of his alter egos forever.

But pain is never only private. On the contrary, it inexorably makes itself public. And, implacably, the fury of our *Gaddus*, as he liked to call himself, wields his axe on his own country – the same country he is willing to defend with his life – on its people and on its governments. Written from the somewhat uncomfortable observation post of the trenches and the war camps, his *Giornale di guerra e di prigionia* pierces the veil of patriotic rhetoric, in a true and excruciatingly painful act of love. Having acquired knowledge of his state of mind and feeling, this Hamlet of a certain age is now fully equipped to analyse the distortions of a history that is cyclically *out of joint*. Once the breach is made, the torrent is unstoppable. With the passing of time – how much is the question – the collective madness of a 'frenzied people' has consigned the country, *his* country, to a tyrant who 'runs about after women', to 'a hyper-histrionic ham' suffering from 'hereditary violence'.

This new chapter was the ideal sequel to what I had begun years earlier with the performance of those 'lettere luterane e scritti corsari' taken from Pasolini. I decided to present this new work to the public calling it, with Gadda's words, a 'sacred act of knowledge' and handing it over as a secular ritual for a civilised society that wants better for itself – something useful, perhaps, for whoever is now trying to pick up the threads of a country in tatters. In *Eros e Priapo* Gadda writes:

> the crimes of the sad mafia and all those 'enthusiasts' of crime having reached or rather permeated every imaginable form of pragma, that is, each recess of the Italian system (with a blanket penetration, oh! yes, really), it is obvious that all our cognitive activities and the universal functions of the soul must intervene in the judgement of evil suffered and evil committed.

Such pained words invite hope, I believe, because 'the sacred act of knowledge with which we have to redeem ourselves' may already be 'a sign of the resurrection, if a resurrection is possible from such horrendous wreckage'.

Translated by Christopher John Ferguson

'And what is your environment?'
'My environment is more or less the universe:
the totality of time and the totality of space.'
Carlo Emilio Gadda

Introduction

Federica G. Pedriali

There is something about Gadda. The press is in no doubt, in the wake of box office success: 'Tutti pazzi per Gadda'. The Italian newspaper *Repubblica* cannot hold back: 'That monologue is our mirror' (7 February 2012, pp. 58–9). It is good to know that the nation in tatters still tolerates the mirror. It is even better, for those who are militant about culture, that it should be Gadda, our most exuberant modernist writer, to provide the emergency rations. One hundred and twenty-one performances in two seasons have not just fuelled huge media interest: they do make an urgent statement of the collective need. Denmark, after all, was once the prison, and from there Hamlet, the most isolated, the most singular of us all, indeed spoke to us all. Past and present-day Italy has got plenty of the desperate global place about it. From this latest immortal theatre, from the Italian-ness of the world as it were, our utterly compromised writer – traumatised First World War veteran, diligent supporter of the fascist regime and daring experimentalist of negation – handles the specifics of his times, soil and anthropology in the rabid hope to be able one day to serve as man and citizen. The message couldn't be more serious or more suited to our present world circumstances; there is none of the lightness of postmodernity in pre-postmodernist Gadda. And now, Italy's best kept literary secret is even packaged for emergency export – thank goodness for the visionariness of those resisting in the world of the arts.

Here, however, we also hit our problem. Expert opinion has it, in fact, correctly, that the practicalities of circulation have been decidedly awkward for this writer, overall and in all languages, including Italian, and with English lagging particularly behind, as if the Anglophone system couldn't benefit from exposure to this modernism for specific additional reasons. *Gadda Goes to War* challenges such notions by capitalising on its logistics as one of the Edinburgh Gadda Projects and by producing a new first English translation – that of Fabrizio Gifuni's original drama – as part of a complete Gadda starter-pack designed for an English-speaking audience.

In this way and by selective translational provocations around our emergency, we introduce Italy's greatest modernist writer from five key perspectives – Circulation, Translation, Staging, World-making and Resources – with further scholarly back-up coming through a themed Global Glossary, an Appendix on Gadda's sensorial fascism and an extensive Bibliography. The English translation is presented in Part II of the book with facing Italian, and is accompanied by the DVD of the Italian performance with English subtitles. The resulting tool – both flexible teaching/learning aid and compact companion-style gateway into state-of-the-art criticism on our author – fills a gap in the current provision by relaunching provision altogether.

A new principle, a new dissemination concept, we feel, needed to be explored in this instance, as Gadda challenges all available existing research formats, forcing one to take the initiative in the otherwise settled business of resourcing others through scholarly activities. This is what the Edinburgh Gadda Projects have been about for the last twelve years. And this is why, having tested the potential for circulation of this latest primary Gadda through an integrated public engagement programme comprising the UK premiere of the show, *Gadda Goes to War* is set to exploit the general timeliness of the crisis of everything to make the case for the superior toughness of the creative message, inviting to trust the state of red alert Gadda spins about life and about public life especially.

Fabrizio Gifuni states, rather wonderfully, in connection with the show: 'They have fouled our country. Let's take it back. Let's surprise them through our love for our work.' Gadda, for his part, is all about the joy of labour, as subject, and the duty not to rest, not to give in. There is no relenting, no gratification, for himself or for us, as readers, as he collapses thinking, reading, sharing, circulating news, producing knowledge. Any human record, under his treatment, will give away the Plot, the universal emergency of the particular, of singularity caught as mere extension between two fraudulent Cartesian axes. It was indeed time someone took this energy bar out of the tin box of specialist circulation, translated it within present-day politics and passed it around to the larger Italian public under that excuse – out of the text box, to scores of theatres, to mount a daring provocation to Italy as nation and to all nations as Italy, failed fatherlands and impostor mother tongues, in one and across the board.

Perhaps unsurprisingly, *Gadda Goes to War* turns out to be a militant book, in the name of the militance of this and of all literature. It certainly expects its readers to be fully warned, mobilised and aware that the going to battle is now over to them.

PART I

Circulation

Cristina Olivari and Federica G. Pedriali

Carlo Emilio Gadda (1893–1973) has been called Italy's greatest (and perhaps only) modernist author. His work has been compared to that of Joyce, Céline, Kafka, Conrad, Musil, the major names associated with this transnational movement. Yet he is also routinely presented as quintessentially Italian, Lombard and above all Milanese. This extremely wide spectrum of definition seems to fit Gadda's writing indeed rather well: an author of all-embracing digressions and painstaking descriptions, he is forever reaching out to the infinitely big and the infinitely small.

Inevitably, critics have been drawn to comparison when dealing with his works, whether to propose it, oppose it, or deny its very possibility, while at the same time casting him as a literary *unicum*. The discipline has come a long way since Gianfranco Contini's initial comparison with macaronic Renaissance poet Teofilo Folengo, in the 1930s and 1940s (Contini 1989: 3, 55). The network of affinities across the canons of world literature – from the early modern irregulars (Bruno, Cervantes, Swift and Sterne) to the French and Russian realists (Balzac, Flaubert, Dostoevsky) to transitional postmodernists and postmodernists proper (Beckett, Nabokov, Pynchon) – has been carefully and extensively explored over the years. Rather surprisingly, then, given the comparative bite of this fiction and the qualifiers – baroque, macaronic, *pasticheur*, experimental, modernist, postmodernist – invoked to describe it, Gadda's international circulation, especially his circulation in English, has not yet come to the fore as a subject of study, despite having definitely emerged as something of an issue.

Reception is an extremely broad term – so broad, in fact, that a whole discipline has developed around it. The reception of any cultural import, of literature more specifically, is a complex matter. All sorts of variables and factors play a role in the process, and many of these are difficult, if not impossible, to retrace, let alone analyse. The historical, cultural and political contexts of both the source and the receiving systems and their reciprocal power relations; the status of literature, and of translated literature more specifically, in the cultures involved; the motives, affiliations and actions of the various agents of import and export, publishing houses, editors, scholars, pundits and translators; the fluctuating inclusion in the literary canons of the day, also as a result of extra-literary considerations, both at home and abroad; not to mention educational policies, national curricula and the day-to-day decisions of educational practitioners – for is the subject really suitable for teaching, examining, setting theses? This is what produces exposure, acquisition, sales figures, circulation and, ultimately, long-term reception.

One thing is sure and reiterated when it comes to Gadda. Circulation both in Italy and abroad, especially the latter, is a real challenge, particularly so the circulation in English. The Anglophone market is vast, extremely profitable and culturally powerful. Yet only around three per cent of publications in the UK and the US at present are translations. With limited opportunities available, the foreign titles that make it into the coveted English market are very few. Given the odds, experimental twentieth-century literature is bound to be difficult to place and to promote. Gadda's works, however, have been translated and studied, in English, as well as in many other languages, and this has taken place despite the most enduring and most pervasive of the available critical tenets: his fundamental *untranslatability*. His unconquerable *Italianness*.

This is why with the present volume we are producing not just a new first English translation, but also a translation *plus*, supporting Gadda in foreign guise through a number of dissemination platforms packed in one. If we are to engage distant audiences, we must address the problem we have: a problem primarily but not exclusively of settled convictions, of receptions already shaped and by now fairly resilient to change, and this regarding not just Gadda but also what constitutes, what deserves to constitute the exportable Italian literary canon. When it comes to the twentieth-century, why indeed discover or rediscover Gadda for that matter when Calvino, Eco, Lampedusa, Levi, Morante, Moravia, Pirandello, Svevo, Tabucchi, even Pasolini satisfy most foreign expectations?

Though the issue may be viewed as academic, here it will not receive a purely academic treatment – the opportunity is too great. Fabrizio Gifuni's original intersemiotic translation from text to performance, tested as it was recently through the further physical transfer to

Edinburgh as part of the UK premiere of the show, challenges somewhat static, reiterated notions of Gadda's difficulty and untranslatability, his allegedly intransitive content and stylistic excess. Travelling books and circulating literature simply do not happen without the investment of institutions and people, what sociologists call agents of communication and circulation. This is the complex affair we want to address by equipping *L'ingegner Gadda va alla guerra* for the journey to distant shores and shelves. Translations are the first step in an author's circulation, and Gadda is no exception: they are physical objects that exist somewhere else, somewhere distant from the author's home, from his language and culture. Carrying defamiliarisation within, translations look for pundits in overseas shops and libraries and from the desks of foreign editors and journalists, also paving the way for non-native professional criticism to arise. Yes, critics and then scholars come to play the other, the complementary key factor, in a reception story, both at home and abroad. The critics' seal of approval is essential to make foreign publishers take the sizeable financial risk of investing in a foreign title. Once the risk is taken and the translation is available, critics, scholars and intellectuals are then called upon to give their view, to praise or attack, accept or reject. The whole process represents, in a way, the biorhythm of circulation and acceptance, what theorists have called the collective construction of an author's image, and images are powerful things.

What, then, of the image in question? The tags have been there, activated and in full working order, right from the start. We too listed them straightaway – baroque, macaronic, *pasticheur*, experimental, modernist, postmodernist – always remembering to name the ultra-local element also, thus bringing in the qualifiers of the ultra-singular, of the *unique* writer as well. And yet, if we start digging into this heavily tagged reception story, the facts of a real and quite successful circulation are there as well. In post-Second World War Italy, for instance, in a context, that is, where selling fifteen thousand copies was a hit, Gadda's *Quer pasticciaccio brutto de via Merulana* (1957 – *That Awful Mess on Via Merulana*, 1965) was indeed a best-seller and one that brought its author into the spotlight of the Italian cultural scene turning him into a literary celebrity of sorts. The first ever Gadda translation, into German, followed suit – 1961, *Die grässliche Bescherung in der Via Merulana*, by Toni Kienlechner. It was, however, the international community of the literati that set the ball of Gadda's international circulation rolling.

In 1963, Gadda's other major novel *La cognizione del dolore* (*Acquainted with Grief*, 1969) won the prestigious Prix International

de Littérature. Gadda's name thus appeared in the same roll as Saul
Bellow and Luis Borges, *ex-aequo* winners, two years earlier, of the
first edition of the prize, then named Prix international des éditeurs.
And sure enough, international *éditeurs* did not fail to spot the opportunity for a new prestigious addition to their catalogues of what today
is known as world literature. Throughout the 1960s, *Quer pasticciaccio*, the disruptive crime novel set in an outrageous fascist Rome, and
La cognizione, the story of a contemporary Hamlet negating Italy from
a fake South America, were translated into many languages – French,
German, Spanish, Rumanian, Czech, Serbo-Croat and Greek, among
others – and more interestingly for us into English. From then on, some
literary markets have taken to Gadda more than others, translating
more and more consistently throughout the decades, while others have
produced only a handful of volumes. To date, the French catalogue
is the most inclusive, with twenty-six published translations. Gadda's
works are currently available in fifteen languages, including Japanese,
Hebrew, Polish and Slovenian; Danish is just about to be added to the
list through the forthcoming first translation of *La cognizione* by Conni
Kay Jørgensen. The two major novels, *Pasticciaccio* and *Cognizione*,
remain the most translated, with thirteen translations each in print, plus
one retranslation, one recent Spanish re-edition and the first Danish
translation just mentioned in the pipeline for the latter.

In the wake of the Prix, in the same year of the Prix actually, the
Italian literary magazine *Europa letteraria* devoted a special issue to this
exciting new name. Right from the title, *Gadda europeo* aimed to place
our author in a continental dimension; among the critics and translators
contributing to the issue, French intellectual Michel Butor focused in
particular on Gadda's so-called *tragic incompleteness* (Butor 1963), an
image destined to continue to stir controversy to this day. Critical circulation was also beginning to work both ways, with foreign critics writing
in Italian and Italian scholars working in other languages (Fusco 1963;
Pucci 1967); the first non-Italian monograph was published in German
by the end of the decade (Gersbach 1969). Should there still be any
doubt about Gadda's transnational appeal, it is promptly swept away
by the somewhat hard fact that this supposedly unwieldy author has
been critiqued in at least ten languages, including Polish, Catalan and
Danish. It is also worth noting that the critical bibliography in English is
not only rich, varied and valuable – it is, more significantly, the largest
one in languages other than Italian.

In short, through the combined provocation of *Pasticciaccio*, primarily at first in the Italian cultural arena, and *Cognizione*, mostly as

a result of the award of the Prix, since the 1960s Gadda's works have travelled far and wide beyond Italy and the Italian language, a journey essentially initiated by translators and scholars. Against rather unadventurous claims of untranslatability periodically reinforced from a variety of quarters, this author too has been *trans*-lated, in the original sense of the word, moving and being moved to new places and new conditions. Gadda's unique tangle of languages and dialects, archaisms and neologisms, his clashing styles and challenging syntax and, crucially, his profoundly local settings, themes and voices – whether Lombard-Milanese, Latian-Roman or *simply* Italian – have certainly not precluded his works from travelling across schools of thought, and more importantly, across linguistic and cultural boundaries. On the contrary, his idiosyncratic individuality, together with his deep universal insight on life, death, order, knowledge, justice, politics, sexuality and chaos, to name but a few basics, have made him the opposite of provincial, of *untranslatable*. From the vantage point of his critical (and translational) circulation, Carlo Emilio Gadda emerges in fact as a truly *glocal* author: a literary great with the rare ability to write locally (Italian-ly), and think globally (universally).

It is time we zoom in on the English Gadda. This story within the story spans nearly five decades and two continents, and involves three publishers, five translators, several renowned scholars, one research centre in Edinburgh, plus one Italian dramatist/actor – all of which revolving around one exceptional author. Let's start from the chronology – 1964: the first English translation. New literature is often best sampled in short story format. As a parody of plastic-spastic futurist writing, 'L'incendio di via Keplero' (first published 1940 – AG RR II 699–713; translated as 'The fire on Via Keplero') was indeed very short and immensely appealing in its stylistic flair. The agent (the facilitator) was, again, the Prix. William Weaver was then an American in Rome. He had been part of the American Field Service in Italy during the Second World War, and having fallen in love, as they say, with the country, had returned, after completing his degree at Princeton in 1946, with the youthful intent of 'becoming a writer' (Spiegelman 2002). Not that he did know Gadda or the unfolding *caso Gadda*, but he was asked to translate this emerging author for the magazine *Art and Literature* (Weaver 1999: 33).

1965: the major, the official first English translation. As further proof that the Anglophone system was part and parcel of Gadda's first wave of near mainstream international success, American publisher George Braziller commissioned the translation of *Pasticciaccio*, and it was

Weaver this time providing the link. Again, a few individuals became packed with agency, with the power to make or break. Weaver was becoming acquainted with Gadda and his younger scholar friend (and later biographer) Gian Carlo Roscioni, and worked closely with them in Rome, where the author by then lived. He later remembered submitting queries to Gadda, who would often 'in his shy, but imposing manner, dismiss the problem, saying simply "cut that"'. Weaver would then turn to Roscioni, 'who could almost always offer the solution himself and, frequently, overcome Gadda's prickly reluctance to reveal his meanings' (Weaver 1989: 123). The resulting *Awful Mess* in Weaver's words was a 'daunting but infinitely rewarding' enterprise (*That Awful Mess*, 1984: xxi). It must have been a fairly successful investment, too, for Braziller, since the firm hired Weaver to translate the other major novel, *La cognizione del dolore*, soon after. Weaver's *Acquainted with Grief* appeared four years later, in 1969.

Braziller's strategy – translate first *Pasticciaccio*, then do *Cognizione* – made a lot of sense, including the business side of things. *Pasticciaccio* had not yet made it to international fame, and even in Italy its popularity was not free from controversy. Yet this singular writer with two very different and nearly antagonistic major novels in his pocket could polarise and divide, not just the public, but also – and this is what matters most to a publisher – the publishing industry. Giulio Einaudi (publisher of *Cognizione*) was in fact not winning the contest with Livio Garzanti (publisher of *Pasticciaccio*) over the ownership of Gadda. And how had Garzanti taken the lead? By publishing the detective novel. Here we have, again, by the way, two key individuals, indicating additionally that major investors – the top Italian publishers of the day – were ready to enter the arena of financial risk to secure Gadda's potential for success for their firm.

Garzanti's gamble, back in 1957, was also paying off because of another unique selling point of *Pasticciaccio*. As early as 1959, Pietro Germi, a leading name in the Italian film industry of the day, had adapted Gadda's crime novel for the big screen and produced the film *Un maledetto imbroglio*, taking the main role alongside Claudia Cardinale. Then like now, there could hardly be a better seal of popularity for a work of fiction. And if this wasn't enough, Braziller, the foreign investor, could also play the card of the investigation set in Rome, the *caput mundi* until recently ruled by the disgraced fascist regime which America had brought to its knees; all of this could be implicitly packed into the product. In sum, Braziller's decision makes the fullest of sense. Translate the popular and antifascist Roman novel first. Rome, crime, politics and

sex, or anyway sexuality, are the eternal attractors. The genre, the politics, the plot, the city . . . by the winner of the Prix, etc. etc., in expectation of the critically acclaimed and differently antifascist – message twice
reinforced – *Cognizione*. These were powerful selling points then, just
as they would be now. Their sum total, including a very definite Germi
effect, were ideally suited to prepare the Anglophone public for a more
difficult tale: one more evidently affected by that obscure sickness of the
contemporary subject which, back in Italy, had already inspired both the
next generation's experimental provocation – the avant-garde Gruppo
63 – and the innermost explorations of the diseased self – Giuseppe
Berto's 1964 major title *Il male oscuro*.

As Weaver pointed out in his introduction, *Cognizione* was an
altogether different beast, and this from a translational point of view
alone. The task may have looked linguistically less challenging while
still being unmistakeably Gaddian, but the effort required by a brand
new set of stylistic complexities was, again, quite formidable. The technicalities of the translation process do not interest us here. Weaver's
Cognizione – this is what matters to us – is a unique case in Gadda's
circulation overall, both national and international, for reasons other
than translational strategies or stylistic solutions. Written and cir-
culated in instalments in the literary magazine *Letteratura* between
1938 and 1941, immediately after his mother's death and well before
Pasticciaccio, *Cognizione* was Gadda's first published novel. It was in
its first volume edition from Einaudi 1963, following the success of
Pasticciaccio from Garzanti 1957, that it had earned Gadda the Prix
International. However, this same edition was also, by Gadda's own
admission, unfinished. His coffers of rejected, self-censored *scraps* have
since become legendary – all the more so as they continue to reveal material to this day, forty years since the author's death, in 1973. In the case
of *Cognizione* the most explosive section of the book was missing. In
the last part of the novel (Part III in the English translation), the mother
(very much Gadda's mother, within very much Gadda's own story,
despite the highly improbable South American setting) suffers a brutal
attack in her own home. She is left dying and suspecting her own son,
thus adding a new, even deeper and darker level to the story.

It is this section that makes *Acquainted with Grief* special. Gadda
gave permission to publish this final part to Braziller first, and Weaver
translated the missing pages straight from the manuscript. The following
year, an extended edition was published in Italian, but it is a real and
hard fact that the full version of Gadda's masterpiece was published first
in English. Now this world exclusive is much more than a good piece of

trivia. Gadda was notoriously reluctant to give away, literally, his works; this was another way not to surrender their meaning. In many respects extremely prolific, he kept most of his writings to himself; very little, come to think of it, had been published by the time of his death. Several major works, starting from the philosophical treatise *Meditazione milanese* (written in 1928 but published in 1974, SVP 615–894) and the first attempted novel *Racconto italiano di ignoto del novecento* (1924–5 but published 1983, SVP 381–613), have been released only in death. Gadda was obsessed with not causing trouble, to others and above all to himself, and was constantly wary that his works could be used in evidence in a trial, his part in the process being, invariably, that of the wrongly accused – *L'ingegner Gadda va alla guerra* bears witness to this compulsion to testify. Clearly, letting go, indeed very publicly, of the last section of *Cognizione*, where his alter ego Gonzalo could be suspected of matricide, must have been a tough decision to take. Yet our Gadda-Hamlet does let go, and chooses Weaver, and the English market, in which to do so. The distant translation to such foreign parts as New York and London, for someone as involved in his work as Gadda, may have helped bridge the gap to a removed confession and to coming clean at last. Foreign words, spent among foreign hands and minds, far from the cruel gaze of one's own people, are no longer ours somehow. Still, and more prosaically perhaps, Gadda's choice also reveals a certain level of trust in the translator and the publisher, on the one hand; on the other, it shows an active interest on Weaver's and Braziller's part in bringing a more special and more exclusive Gadda to the forefront of the international circulation.

But now be ready for the set-back. For what else is there? More specifically, what has happened to the English Gadda since 1969? French readers can enjoy twenty-six volumes in translation; German enthusiasts have got access to ten. The subject has flourished academically, in English as well as in several other languages. However, the translation we are presenting in this book is only the fourth to have been published in single volume since Weaver's groundbreaking work. By 1999, American scholar Robert de Lucca began to express concern regarding what had been translated into English and when, also arguing that one needed to understand why the English Gadda had not taken off. While in fact in continental Europe Gadda was firmly established as 'the giant among Italy's modern prose writers', his reception, we could say his circulation, in the Anglophone context had 'not been a success' (de Lucca 2002: 133). Guilty as charged, the existing English translations: in de Lucca's view, Weaver's efforts, particularly his version of *Pasticciaccio*, were so 'inadequate' as to impact negatively on the author's fortune in English. Weaver's *Mess*, in sum, failed to convey Gadda's lexical variety and density of expression, in other words the very features that made his work worth reading, studying and circulating. Weaver's alleged banalisation and medium register particularly struck de Lucca as ultimately anti-Gaddian, and he did not refrain from criticism, particularly in his 2002 paper. As a matter of fact, Weaver's standardising strategy could be justified precisely in terms of circulation, namely as a way to facilitate reception by bringing Gadda closer to the English reader – any reader. But the critique was coming from an academic position: Weaver's translations were inadequate from a critical-philological point of view, and one had to set this right first. For this reason, de Lucca did not limit himself to an act of translational *j'accuse*, however detailed and reasoned. He went on to offer what he saw as the solution: a retranslation of *Pasticciaccio*. Before we move on to consider that work – what survives of it – a look at what was happening to Gadda in his other translational journeys might help to put the alleged English inadequacy or failure into perspective.

At the time of de Lucca's critique of Weaver's translations, the English Gadda had been practically dormant for thirty years, while the German and especially the French translational processes had just achieved their two most productive decades to date. In Germany, the 1980s saw three new translations hit the markets, and the 1990s topped the charts with seven. In France, the dynamism of the Gadda system in the same two decades is even more marked: twenty-one new translations were produced between 1980 and 1999, evenly distributed between the 1980s (eleven) and the 1990s (ten). These data allow at least two important observations. Firstly, it is not translation itself that is somehow inadequate in the case of Gadda, or that Gadda is per se untranslatable. The French and German systems seem to have coped well with the process. Secondly, de Lucca's frustration was understandable – the Anglophone system had definitely been left behind. Yet, blaming one agent as *the* agent, acquitting all other parties involved in Gadda's reception and circulation, scholarly criticism included, is something of a flawed argument and surely less acceptable.

Extracts from de Lucca's *Awful Mess* began to appear in 1999, strictly in academic publications (they are now also available in *The Edinburgh Journal of Gadda Studies* as a taster of a different *Mess*). The translator's academic background and target audience seep through his pages. With detailed footnotes and frequent borrowings from the Italian, this *Pasticciaccio* is close to what in translation studies is known as a thick translation, one that aims to place the target text within a rich multi-layered cultural context. Unfortunately, de Lucca's attempt to address the English translational hiatus was cut short by an untimely demise – a sad reminder that literature needs real agents to circulate successfully. On the other hand, his work appeared when interest was on the up in the European academic circles, this time including the United Kingdom and Edinburgh in particular.

Putting it differently still. With full canonisation achieved and marked, back home, through the publication of the complete works (1988–93) and the centenary celebrations (1993), the Italian consensus was that internationalisation in this case would remain primarily academic and based on fairly small numbers of expert users. From the start, the research carried out from Edinburgh has instead been marked by the opposite conviction. Gadda could be successfully embedded in the curriculum (1997: first Honours course ever taught in the UK, suitably catalogued under the title *Cleaning up the 'Mess'*). His proto-hypertextual syntax could be adopted and showcased through the new web media (2000: *The Edinburgh Journal of Gadda Studies* gets established under Federica Pedriali's direction). The subject could be developed and championed through purpose-built e-platforms (2002, 2004, 2008: *A Pocket Gadda Encyclopedia*, in-progress online editions, with forthcoming print edition in four volumes). *The Edinburgh Gadda Journal*, *EJGS* for short, has since become the third most popular web resource in our College generating 7.3 per cent of all Humanities traffic to the University's server (2007: national statistics produced by University College London). If this makes Edinburgh the premier centre for the promotion of Gadda studies worldwide, what we are establishing here by reporting these data is not so much about Edinburgh but about Gadda and his very real potential for broad-spectrum internationalisation. An average 300,000 to 400,000 hits per year do not happen either by chance or through specialist user traffic. Access levels of this kind are simply exceptional for the Humanities, let alone for a single-author resource, and require, beyond the requirements of governments and research assessment exercises, that scholars adjust their perception of the subject's broader appeal for the general public.

The Edinburgh initiative, for its part, has adapted through growth and the exploration of growth potential. Established in the *EJGS* decennial (2010), the Edinburgh Gadda Prize has, for instance, radically extended the journal's original remit, making Edinburgh the catalyst for *real* and *local* – in addition to *virtual* and *global* – community engagement around the complex affair of Gadda's wider circulation. Through the junior categories of the Prize, through the first Italian edition, Gadda Giovani 2011, in particular, what has been tested and exported – from Edinburgh to Italy and back – is a circulation formula that capitalises on active collaboration with the performing arts to back up scholarly dissemination efforts in the wider community. This, luckily, means once again individuals, as the Milan Finals of Gadda Giovani 2011 amply demonstrated, from a packed 500-seater Franco Parenti Theatre, the very stage of Amleto Pirobutirro's debut, back in January 2010, this time shared by Fabrizio Gifuni with our fourteen national finalists. On these first major results, Edinburgh 2012, the third edition of the Prize, pulled off a further series of firsts under the programmatic title *Gadda è teatro | Scholarship is engagement*, including the first postgraduate summer school *Gaddus Scholars* and the first international Gadda Juniors mobility project, as well as the UK premiere of *L'ingegner Gadda va alla guerra*. Montecassino 2013 and London 2014 will follow, and the present volume will be on site on such occasions as part of the combined advocacy by increasingly hybrid circulation means.

Virtual and real engagement: with proactive acts of export and import. A kind of 360° commitment to the subject, along the all too linear axis of a reality principle that so far has only allowed to realise as much – but also, how much. Some will argue, possibly quite rightly, that the fact that such efforts are needed only prove the point of the impossible, of the unsustainable quality of the Gadda phenomenon – just like the latest philological feats, by Gadda's newest agent of investment, Adelphi Edizioni, Gadda's main publisher since 2010. Paradoxically, in fact, without the editors and the philologists pushing the rescue of this rotund-explosive messy-architectural writing, there would not be Gadda and hence no scholarly exclusive on Gadda. Similarly, without Edinburgh forcing both the local and distant globe to note how much can be done despite what appears to be the toughest possible dissemination task, there wouldn't be the flourishing global circulation that there ultimately is. Yes, this complex Gadda affair is indeed circular – but would we rather not have it?

The lesson, if the register can be forgiven, is that agents of circulation are not to blame for their agency, even if it happens to challenge already settled collective persuasions over matters of cultural worth. Is Gadda worth it? Or rather, is the effort required by his promotion worth our efforts? As stated already, the opportunity to ask this question again, in English, was there and not to be missed. The tremendous mental effort that has produced *L'ingegner Gadda va alla guerra* had to extend as

Gadda Goes to War, and further still as *Gadda è teatro | Scholarship is engagement*. It had to come to this book *plus*, in an additional act of translation placing the original Italian show, i.e. the original inter-semiotic transfer from text to stage, at a further bustling intersemiotic junction. This is what is meant, technically, with a translation *plus*, and what it comprises is not just discreet units (text, translation, intersemiotic translation, original criticism, with further back-up also in DVD form and though new live performance). In this venture, agents (people) have supported the text to achieve its translation via combined (and collective) translational strategies involving an extended number of agents (other people), platforms (such as public engagement initiatives) and complementary outcomes (including scholarly events and their further outputs), and resulting in the *text* feeding back as *texts* (performance, translation, illustration, subtitles, surtitles, criticism) to its beneficiaries (again but not conclusively, *people*).

This latest Edinburgh initiative is certainly unique in the history of Gadda studies. For the Edinburgh Gadda Group, now also affectionately known as the Gifuni Group, turning the opportunity that was too great into a captivating physical agent of further global circulation has also meant a highly valuable early career training experience, as our contributors profiles also confirm. Out of the unique and even necessary isolation in which most scholarly work gets done, we have built an enriched and enriching connectivity of agents engaging, indeed almost militantly, with our task, in the name of Gadda's future. We trust that this privileged instant in the infinite archive of human endeavour, having passed through Gadda and now also passing through Edinburgh (its server, its University Press, its postgraduate students), will continue to win the one argument without which the world would be a very sad place. The argument that has been our motto throughout the many stages of this work – *si può fare!*

Endnote

This chapter makes use of notions and approaches from translation studies. The role of translation in the circulation of literature is a major focus for Lefevere (1992). Translation as circulation agent, initially taken by translation studies from sociology, is presented in its many aspects in Milton and Bandia (2009: 1–18). Developing Genette's seminal *Paratexts* (1997), scholars in translation studies have also focused on the role of paratexts in translated literature – among the most interesting contributions, see Watts (2000) and Tahir-Gürçağlar

(2002). Finally, the idea of thick translation was advanced in relation to de Lucca's retranslation of *Pasticciaccio*. Appiah (1993) was the first to introduce this translational strategy and translational agenda.

The third English translation was not discussed as part of this chapter, despite mention of an English Gadda in four volumes. The *Philosophers' Madonna* (original Italian title *La Madonna dei Filosofi*, 1928, then 1931, MdF RR I 69–107) appeared in 2008, this time published by Atlas Press, London. Atlas is a small independent publisher that specialises in twentieth-century experimental fiction, with a focus on France (the translator himself, Antony Melville, normally works from English into French). The book is a slim eighty-page long paperback edition of a fairly conventional short story. (In the first magazine edition, 1928, before it became the title of Gadda's first short prose collection, 1931, the complete wording included the parenthetic qualifier *Novella borghese*.) Inevitably, given the choice of text, translation no. 3 cannot compare with either Weaver's classic or de Lucca's partial retranslations. However, this was the first single-volume translation to appear in English since 1969, and the first ever to be entirely originated in the UK, possibly in the wake of the active British scene of recent years – in short and all considered, a highly positive development. It was also with this translation in mind that, when the opportunity that could be great presented itself through the collaboration between Fabrizio Gifuni and Federica Pedriali, the translation project, which like the encyclopedia and the prize had been among the *things to do next* since 2000, became that of a translation *plus*, on and around an actual translation task of small proportions. In this case, in fact, small proportions could have significant implications, given the poignancy that the former acquire when handled by agents, like Gifuni, ready to commit whatever single-minded vision it takes to bring a project to fruition – one of the most uncanny things there are. This is to say that Gadda's next chance in the Anglophone market goes back, ultimately, to an Italian dramatist/actor's choice of text: a choice originally made for the local (national) scene, and now fortified with the decision to take this compact existential emergency ration to where it can speak, literally and nearly, to us all.

Translation

Christopher John Ferguson

The job of translating Gadda is one that cannot be taken lightly. William Weaver – the translator's translator – once remarked, 'especially in translating Gadda, there are no perfect solutions. You simply do your best' (Weaver 1989: 120). It was with this commandment – to do my best – ringing in my ears that I embarked on this translation.

Luckily, this is not a case of the translator working alone. Cristina Olivari is another enthusiastic student of Gadda, and we saved each other immeasurable amounts of time and effort by combining expertise and knowledge of the foibles of our respective *madrelingue*. It is the first time I have collaborated so directly with someone on a translation project and I must say it was an experience that I would definitely like to repeat.

This was also the first time we had worked with a CAT programme in an attempt to produce a translation that is more consistent, bearing in mind that we were dealing with the fusion of two disparate texts by the same author. A computer-assisted translation, such as the one we produced using the open source programme OmegaT, is not the same as machine translation (this is what Google Translate and BabelFish do). The software in this case analyses your translation as you write, remembering when certain word strings were translated in certain ways before. Other features that ensure accuracy include formatting tags and sentence-by-sentence breakdown of the source text. Not that it was always desirable to take the software's suggestions, but it was good to have the information at hand in an organised way. Gadda constantly revisits the same concepts, conceits and words, and this was something that we had to preserve.

L'ingegner Gadda va alla guerra is filtered, interpreted Gadda. Fabrizio Gifuni has disassembled and reaggregated two primary texts, *Giornale di guerra e di prigionia* and *Eros e Priapo*, also interpolating two discarded fragments from *La cognizione del dolore* and lines from *Hamlet*. This resulting new work is what provided the context and the blueprint for a first English translation of the primary Gadda, which is what we have produced. Gifuni opens the play by quoting Shakespeare. For once, this is a great situation for the translator of Gadda into English to be in because it sets a register that the audience will immediately recognise as being literary and theatrical. Shakespeare is eloquent, elegant, difficult even, but crucially he is also a great innovator of English and grabs the attention of the English-speaking reader in a very specific way. In picking the Shakespeare-in-Gadda to provide the framework for a new Gadda for the stage, Gifuni has not only set a theatrical tone and elevated his material to the level of the Bard (the reader's expectations cannot but be high right from the outset, given the exhibited intertext). Implicitly, he has also elevated the translator, especially the translator into English, who is being offered, shall we say, a similar mantle. This then establishes the tone for what follows in more ways than one, and more important still, it sets the translator free to innovate, to *translate* – a rare thing judging from the scarcity of English translations of our author.

Gadda is a writer who loves to jump between high and low registers, sometimes lyrical and sometimes satirical, sometimes eschatological and sometimes scatological. By common critical consent, it is in this jumble of styles that Gadda finds his own style, and reflecting both the high and low was something that we as translators were very conscious of. To give a couple of examples, the closing monologue of the first section of the play is rather involved as well as abstract and philosophical in style. It does not actually come from the *Giornale di guerra e di prigionia* – it is one of the discarded compositional notes for the later *Cognizione del dolore*:

> [. . .] e la volontà di bene, la rinuncia, la pena profonda: vedute solo da Dio, dal fondo abissale di quel suo cazzioso caleidoscopio.

The entire fragment is a difficult one, especially because we are trying to engage the audience after they have read lines and extemporisation on lines from *Hamlet* and maintain the theatrical effect. We are also in a position where we must handle our readers with care, given that their expectations for the piece are only now beginning to form. We found the whole of this passage challenging, but this selection presented special difficulties. Firstly, the sentence, which starts with a nominal clause ('Senza stagione la vita, e senza gioia: [. . .]'), after the punctuation mark reopens with 'and', not a particular problem and common enough in spoken language, but then there follows a list – we will speak more of lists later – no main verbs in sight for a while, and this is difficult to put effectively into English. We must decide whether in English it will be possible to maintain the rhythm and the syntactical aspect of the sentence while also listing the nouns: 'the will of / for Good(ness), the renouncement, the deep pain' is a possible first draft, but there are a number of obvious problems: the ambiguity of the first item, the word *renouncement* which is unusual and, to my ears, rather ugly, and the slight cliché of the *deep pain*. In playing around with *renouncement*, however, I stumbled on the idea that *renouncing it* sounded better (yes, certain options do sound better, a serious issue for theory), and set about changing the list of nouns into a sentence. While the *it* lacks the totality of *la rinuncia*, it does bring back something of the abstract referent of the original at the same time allowing the reader to make more sense of the list and making the sentence more plausible in English. This choice, as already hinted, was partly dictated by the position this section appears in, partly by our desire to engage our audience on the right kind of footing from the start. Finally we arrived at:

The yearning for good, renouncing it, the dolorous suffering,

using words like *yearning* and *dolorous* to direct the listener back, to some extent, to the Shakespeare that they had just heard, while also trying to add depth to the feelings expressed, a depth that, in Italian, might be expected to come from the disembodied, unconnected grammar of the list.

The second part of the quotation came out as:

all seen by God alone, from the abysmal bottom of his cantankerous kaleidoscope

in which *abissale* comes neatly into *abysmal*, a word for which the metaphorical meaning has usurped the literal. This will hopefully surprise the listener slightly as an unusual use of a familiar word. *Abissale* does not have the same effect in Italian, but *cazzioso* is certainly unusual. It is close in sound, of course, to *cazzo*, and therefore causes a different kind of mild shock, but it is actually an innocent enough term for something that is prevaricating, mean-spirited, annoyed and annoying. *Cantankerous* covers it well enough, and also has the benefit of sounding old-fashioned, even if it is a word of fairly recent origin (late eighteenth century: see Goldsmith's 'cantankerous toad' in *She Stoops to Conquer*, II, 44, which is effectively theatrical for our purposes). This mix of the old and new is also quite common in Gadda. In fact, this whole problematic excerpt is typical – if such a word can be employed – of the mature Gadda, as much in terms of imagery as language. The Gadda reader will be used in time to this kind of driven philosophical and pseudo-philosophical discourse (it is occasionally difficult to know whether or not to take him seriously) in the form of digressions and extemporisations. *Volontà*, the abyss, *Dio* – mean-spirited and nasty, yet capitalised all the same – are all concepts that Gadda reaches for time and again.

Speaking of the tension between modern and archaic language, there were other moments in which Gadda gives his prose the mock-epic feel by using older forms of Italian:

> Hodie quel vecchio Gaddus e duca di Sant'Aquila arrancò du' ore per via sulle spallacce del monte Faetto, uno scioccolone verde per castani, prati, e conifere, come dicono i botanici, e io lo dico perché di lontano non distinsi se larici o se abeti vedessi . . .

> On this day, Old Gaddus, Duke of Sant'Aquila trudged for two hours up the shoulders of Mount Faetto, a great big green fool, through fields, chest-nuts and coniferophyta, as the botanists say, and I say this because from a distance I could not make out whether they were larches or silver firs.

We notice, naturally, the Latinate *Hodie* and *Gaddus*, and the missing *e* at the end of *du* (two), which to my non-native ear rings more of Florentine Italian than of Subsonica, but we also spot a kind of pedantic exactitude, both in the language and in the content: the 'conifere, come dicono i botanici' and the implied excuse for lack of precision. So we read the sentence as mock-epic or old-fashioned at the least – given that these are again common features in the tangles of Gadda's style – running into scientific jargon infused with a kind of passive-aggressive pedantry. Here, as in so many other places, we failed to fully express this. We tried retaining *hodie*, but it seems balled up more with the names of Latin hymns than any idea of time: 'Hodie Christus natus est', as the carol goes. We had a go with something like 'in this day of the Year of Our Lord 1915', but it came across as too wordy and redundant in a diary entry. Instead, we opted to keep *Gaddus* and capitalise the *old* as if to give an idea of some legendary name. Then we had some debate about the *conifere*. After some consultation, we found that the Italian term is quite marked, allowing us to imply the pedantic nature of the sentence through the apparently needless use of the Latin name of the genus. We also made the decision to change the list order so that the rhythm of the translation was improved.

Already in this first entry from the *Giornale*, the high register – whether lyrical, philosophical or scientific – is soon undercut by mentions of *pidocchi* (lice) and *sputi* (sputum). This is classic Gaddian style, especially because often it is the lowest things that are raised to the highest excesses of his language. Thus *sputum* – accompanying the actor's noisy expectoration – and not *grog*, *lugie* or whatever the local idiom may be. What is interesting is that while Gadda seems quite happy with the vulgar and the bawdy in general, in theory and in the population, he is not so forthcoming in terms of his own bodily functions. Luckily, English has similar evasive techniques to those that Gadda makes use of:

Sto abbastanza bene di corpo

becomes, again rather neatly:

I feel fairly well – in myself

which is precisely the way that my grandmother would have expressed her digestive health, should she have felt the need. Such techniques in spoken language are indeed standard across cultures. The comic effect they generate in Gadda is in clear contrast to his willingness to put everything into his writing, as the reader will appreciate by the time that the sections from *Eros e Priapo* are reached. In this, as in other areas, it has been necessary for me to draw on my experience of English as spoken colloquially in an attempt to represent the full range of the Italian used by Gadda. In my case, this naturally means that Scots is often preferred, and while other translators – notably Weaver – have avoided using localised slang, I saw an opportunity to experiment in certain situations. For example, Mussolini's imagined outburst:

son qua mè, a fò tutt mè a fò tutt mè

caused particular problems. How could we represent the non-standard Italian used in this phrase, how could we maintain the sense of aggression? I also detected a glimmer of comedy in the performance as well, side by side with the violence – a toddler stamping his feet, perhaps, but with uncanny power. A number of possible solutions were proposed: 'I'm here, I'm going to do it all' was, in the end, rejected for missing out on that crucial aggression. A sideways move into Scots-accented English gave us: 'See me, I'm here. See me, I'm going to do it all'. This too was rejected because in this instance the text was not sufficiently marked, and the colloquial use of *see me* is not universally recognisable as an indicator of non-standard English of the Scottish variety. In the end, the whole hog had to be swallowed. The result:

See me? Here, um uh . . . See me? Ah'm awa' tae dae it aw

is still problematic, especially for readers who are unfamiliar with Scots and indeed Glaswegian modes of pronunciation, but it seems an honest and effective attempt to transmit some of the comedy and assertive aggression of the original. I would suggest, if the play is ever going to be performed in English or anyway in languages other than Italian, that the local setting should dictate the register for this moment in the play. At the same time, given the popularity of television programme characters such as Rab C. Nesbitt and Taggart and comedians such as Robert Florence and Kevin Bridges, I think Glaswegian an appropriate idiom for much of the British Isles.

As the play moves into *Eros e Priapo*, the vulgarity increases, as does the lyricism of the language, and we maintained the distinction between the two opposing styles by shifting between a more ornate – Latinate at times – English and a more earthy Scots. For example, the line:

> poiché tutto l'ethos si ha da ridurre alla salvaguardia della loro persona, che è persona scenica e non persona gnostica ed etica, e alla titillazione dei loro caporelli, in italiano capezzoli: e all'augumento delle loro prerogative, per quanto arbitrarie o dispotiche, o tutt'e due

becomes:

> since all ethos must be reduced to protecting their own persona, and that persona is more of a theatrical projection rather than one based on knowledge and ethics, and to titillating their diddies – in English nipples – and expanding their prerogatives, however arbitrary or despotic, or both.

It was with some regret that we rejected *gnostic* as a translation of *gnostica* in favour of *knowledge* – we felt it was, in the end, too closely associated with a particular kind of *gnosis* in English, and incompatible with the idea of simply *knowing*. But elsewhere, the adoption of such Latinate words as *prerogative* and *arbitrary*, and the Greek/French *despotic* gives the required highfalutin tone, a tone which is undermined by the Milanese *caporelli* in Italian and *diddies* in Scots.

A little further on, Gadda uses scientific imagery to discuss the way that the world works:

> [la] Abyssos primigenia: mentre è vero esattamente il contrario: e cioè senza loro la palla de i' mondo la rotola come al biliardo e che Dio esprime in loro il male dialetticamente residuato dalla non-soluzione dei problemi collettivi: essi sono il residuato male defecato dalla storia, lo sterco del mondo . . .

> the primeval Abyssos: while exactly the opposite is true: that without them the ball of the world rolls like a billiard and through them God expresses

the evil that, dialectally, is left behind by the non-solution of collective problems: they are the residual evil defecated by history, the dung of the world.

Here the image of the billiard ball is introduced, a favourite image of the pop scientist, especially in the description of deterministic theories of science. It is interesting that the billiard ball has remained largely the ball of choice, despite the relative popularity of snooker and pool. I have been unable to find out with certainty the first usage of this image, but it dates back to Simon Laplace, the champion of determinism, and it is commonly used today, as a search in scientific journals will show. We decided to omit *ball* from the translation in order to suggest some kind of old-fashionedness, something slightly archaic, as we were unable to replicate the feel of 'palla de i' mondo' above. The billiard ball and the connotations of science influenced our choice later when we came to:

> La voce è richiamo sessuale potente e gravita, per così dire, sull'ovaio alle genti.

Our choice:

> The voice is a powerful sexual attractor and exerts gravity, so to speak, on the ovary of the people

was designed to put the reader or audience in mind of magnets and moons, at least as far as *attractor* and exerting *gravity* were concerned.

One enjoyable – again, if we are permitted such a term – and remarkable feature of Gadda's prose is his predilection for lists. It is a technique that he frequently adopts in the extremes of his famous rages, as if the fabric of language couldn't contain his emotion. The unusual grammar in the lists can often present problems for the translator, as we found in our work. Let us look at an example:

> Asini, asini, buoi grassi, pezzi da grand hotel, avana, bagni; ma non guerrieri, non pensatori, non ideatori, non costruttori; incapaci d'osservazione e d'analisi, ignoranti di cose psicologiche, inabili alla sintesi . . .

> Asses, asses, big fat oxen, grand hotel ninnies, Havana-smokers, watertakers; but not warriors, not thinkers, not inventors, not builders; incapable of observation and analysis, ignorant of psychology, incapable of synthesis.

The important thing, it seemed to us, was to replicate the sense of the list, the meaning of the objects in it, and worry about the violence done to the English language later. In this example, we have the tricky nouns 'pezzi da grand hotel, avana, bagni'. *Pezzi* is difficult to render, with English lacking that meaning for *piece*, leaving us to find a corresponding term. Our choice, *ninnies*, was voted for as a suitably gentle mocking term. *Avana*, which we judged to be a reference to cigars, could only really be rendered as either *cigar smokers* or something similar: in short, we needed the *smoker* part to be made explicit, or go with 'havanas in their mouths', which would have, in our view, broken the flow even more than the extra noun had. The same was the case when it came to *bagni*, although here there was even more room for interpretation. While it might be taken as a sign of their separation from the common soldiers – that is, the generals get to have baths – or as a sign of implied effeminacy, in the style of Boudicca's joshing of the Roman troops, we decided that we would attempt to combine these meanings while also implying a difference in social class. We were thinking of the practice of *taking the waters* at resorts and spas, hence *water-takers*.

Early on in the piece is an example of a word that presented problems disproportionate to its apparent importance in the text: *rosolacci*.

Ahi che le rupi dure e belle del corno Baitone si celavano nelle nubi, forse per ira della non giusta preferenza data ai rosolacci.

To begin with, the text is somewhat difficult to comprehend. In the end, the reading we adopted was that the rocks of the Baitone mountain were somehow offended by the preference that was shown to the flowers on its slopes. This seemed to us to be the only defensible reason, even if it leaves open the question of who this preference was shown by. Was it the troops mentioned just before? People in general? The sun? Some deity? The deity is perhaps the most likely agent of preference in a Gaddian context, given his instinctive reaction towards the problem of evil in a created world – for supporting evidence, see, for instance, *Meditazione milanese* and the chapter 'Il male' (MM SVP 681–97). Yet, even when this shortcoming was settled on as a feature rather than as a fault, we were still left with the difficult *rosolacci*.

One of my favourite tools as a translator is Google's Image search. In those cases where a word is absent from the dictionary, the ability to look at the object described and identify it by sight is a wonderful addition to our toolbox. In this case, however – and this was confirmed by subsequent enquiries and searches – there appear to be two distinct types of plant that this term referred to.

The first was the spiny rose or *rosaccio*, the *ugly rose* (-*accio* being a suffix that, in Italian, indicates ugliness), or rather the wild rose, the rambling rose, that twisted plant that is a feature of town council planting all over the British Isles as much as it is a symbol of the wilderness. To us it is more the plant of the canal towpath than the slopes of mountains. The second was the poppy, the *papaver rhoesas*, which in its over-bloomed state adds an untidy beauty to the fields of Eurasia from the latitude of the Midlands south. Both choices seemed, on the face of it, equally defensible, but each had its own overtones that had to be considered.

Despite its use and its abundance as a plant, as an image, the wild rose is one of romanticism, of great and fragile beauty. It seemed impossible for us to translate *rosolacci* as simply *roses*, so some kind of modifier was required. *Rambling* gave us much the same problem, as well as providing us with an unwelcome alliteration that might lead to an unwanted comic effect, while *ugly roses* or *messy roses* seemed too marked a translation, as if the key was that there was something wrong with the *rosolacci* that caused them to receive the *preference* that the rocks of the Baitone did not.

On the other hand, *poppies* seemed less accurate although backed up by the 1993 French translation of the *Giornale* by Monique Baccelli – translators must check other translations, including translations into languages other than the target language, especially when, as was our case, no previous first translations are available. If Gadda was definitely talking about poppies, why not use *papaveri*? And with us now saying and writing *poppies*, the blousy, over-bloomed image he had *perhaps* intended to evoke with *rosolacci* would also be overwritten by two somewhat static images: the opium poppy – *papaver somniferum* – and the Remembrance Poppy.

This last was a particular problem. The Remembrance Poppy was instituted in the United Kingdom as a memorial of the dead of the First World War, exactly the event that Gadda is describing his part in. However, this poppy is linked to the Western Front, not the Alps, and to the end of the War, following a famous poem *In Flanders' Fields* by a Canadian medic and soldier John McCrae. Perhaps, after all, this would be too strong an image to invoke here, at least for a British audience, for whom the flower itself is almost a national symbol, one that speaks of the futility of war and, simultaneously, of the nobility of the suffering of combatants.

Unfortunately, or perhaps fortunately, translators have, sooner or later, to come to a decision. We have adopted *poppies*, risking that an intended anti-war message be found here, rather than the reader be taken in with romantic notions of delicate wild flowers, trusting that the image created will be the fallow fields of Warwickshire in summer rather than thorny bushes in the middle of a roundabout. Our version:

> Alas! The hard and beautiful rocks of the Baitone concealed themselves in the clouds, perhaps angry at the preference shown unjustly to the poppies

is far from perfection, but after deliberation and discussion, a choice must be made.

There is no room to be squeamish in translating Gadda. While he is, as we have mentioned above, evasive and vague about matters of his own digestion, he is quite happy to decry the subjects of his wrath with sexual and stercoral vehemence. A translator cannot afford to turn away meekly when faced with *Io-minchia*. Meanwhile, we found that Gadda was creative in his insults, with a paradoxical *finesse* that not even we were expecting – and yet, not having expected it, we were more than ready to exploit it. *Cacchio*, an epithet applied to Mussolini, is normally a euphemism for *cazzo*, in the way an English speaker might substitute *feck*, *frick* or *freak* (depending on nationality and accent) for *fuck*. However, *cacchio* is also a botanical term, referring to a sterile branch or offshoot. We decided to go with this uncommon meaning in our translation (*unfruitful shoot*), prompted not only by Gadda's capitalisation of the word, which marks the ultimate singularity of the real item, and by the context – sexual, unsurprisingly – but also by the way he handles the fertility motif more generally. This in fact truly runs riot in the later Gadda, in *Quer pasticciaccio*, that is, and in *Eros e Priapo*. In the former text, for instance, the issue is indeed the distinction between fruitful and unfruitful sexuality, and even more, between legally and illegally fruitful sexuality, ultimately calling into question the legality of everything – not just the local story and the regime, but also history itself, the grand scheme.

We had, in sum, to contend subtly with a great deal of vulgarity, especially when Gadda gets round to talking about Mussolini. While in some places I was pleased with the result that the translation produced ('tutto codesto sfruconare, e cigolare, e anfanare e sudare dipendeva tutto dal kuce: dal Gran Khan!'; 'all that rubbing and creaking and panting and sweating, were all thanks to the Doosh-y: to the Great Khan!'), other attempts seem to lack something, there is some fundamental *dirtiness* missing ('ne la memoria fisica e ne le carni de le Sofronie, al ricordo viscerale del Tauro zefireo'; 'in the physical memory and in the flesh of the Euphemias, to the visceral memory of the life-bringing Bull'). In this last example, perhaps the use of the word *flesh* is sufficiently evocative, and *visceral* might help too, but I cannot say that I am absolutely satisfied that the importance of the Bull is clear to the reader.

Authority figures are always in the front line when Gadda decides to be insulting. Take, for example, the diary entry headed 'Sempre in culo a Cecco Beppo!' We went through a number of variations – 'Up the arse of The Emperor', 'Up your bum, Blind Joe' or even 'Get it round you,

Emperor Franz' were all rejected – before we arrived at the succinct 'Up yours, Franz Josef'. Another example of vulgarity is directed in an even more personal way at Mussolini. He is referred to as *il Kuce*, a rendering of Duce that is intended to show the ignorance of the masses and the meaninglessness that constant repetition of his title brought. We adopted *Doosh-y*, borrowing from the American insult *douche*, a particularly unpleasant epithet; and when Gadda appears to be mocking Mussolini's perceived monstrous largeness before the crowd, we came up with *Moo-so-leeny*, a fine piece of wordplay by my co-translator. That said, it is easy for us to be inventive when insulting Italy's former fascist dictator. Far more problematic for me personally – and this was one part of the translation I did alone – was the translation of racist material in the shape of a song used in the change between the third and fourth scenes in the performance. While this does not appear in the printed translation, it was a necessary part of the subtitling process. The lyrics to the song *L'abissino vincerai* are intended to inspire the Italian soldier to feats of conquest over the Abyssinians: 'Se l'abissino è nero | gli cambierem colore | a colpi di legnate | poi gli verrà il pallore' is a particularly unpleasant example. I found that it is quite one thing to hear or to read racist material and quite another thing to put it into one's own words. It was surprisingly upsetting, and I later abandoned my attempts to revise the phrasing so that it might better suit the marching rhythm of the song. My translation had to be faithful and accurate, but I was not obliged to gild filth. On the other hand, the use of such a piece by Gifuni is not only artistically defensible, it might even be considered a necessity, both from the point of view of condemning the actions and the motives of fascism in Italy – as the theatricalised narrator of *Eros e Priapo* goes on to do in the final two scenes of the play – and from the point of view of honesty as regards Gadda's attitudes towards Africa and Africans, attitudes that might charitably be described as *old-fashioned* and which I would prefer to describe as racist, surely in the period of the Abyssinian invasion. This side of Gadda, however, does not impact on his rabid antifascism, which, following on from the singing of *L'abissino vincerai*, builds up to a furious outpouring in the closing of the play.

In the final section of *L'ingegner Gadda va alla guerra* we see also an increase in the frequency and importance of Christian imagery. This creates a problem for the translator because while Italian Christianity is almost exclusively Catholic-flavoured, the English language has a more protestant bent. Such a seemingly minor point has caught out better translators in the past. For example, Weaver renders *tabernacolo* as *tabernacle* in chapter eight of his translation of *Quer pasticciaccio*, perhaps thinking of the tabernacles of the Baptist and Reformed confessions – small, temporary churches, in essence – when *sanctuary* would perhaps have been better. Certainly, the most common use of the word *tabernacle* in English is for the locked case in which the Blessed Sacrament is kept in a Catholic church, or as the tabernacle of the ark of the covenant as in the Old Testament. With this in mind, we favoured translations that seemed to us to suggest Catholicism rather than any other Christian denomination. Hence *turibolo* is translated as *thurible* rather than the less-loaded *censer*, which would undoubtedly be preferable in a neutral context.

One aspect of the project that was a new experience for us was our adaptation of our translation into subtitles for the DVD of Gifuni's performance of his play. I have already mentioned this in terms of the incidental music that formed part of the production, but it forced our hands in other ways as well. We found that we needed to shorten and simplify the text in places and perhaps to change the word order so that the subtitles might better reflect the image and soundtrack at that moment. In particular, lines that are said rapidly will naturally present more difficulties, forcing a choice to be made between increasing the amount of text on screen, cutting the amount of time text appears or removing words to shorten the translation. The first option could only be used so often: subtitling convention dictates that three-line subtitles may be used occasionally, but four or more lines are not permissible. It is generally considered that this would take up too much in terms of the screen and the viewer's attention. In terms of time on screen, we pushed beyond the boundaries of the 70–80 words a minute recommended by Ofcom for subtitling programmes for the deaf, and instead tested them for readability with non-speakers of Italian. In addition, we made sure that the *quick-change* subtitles were one line in length. Finally, we simplified the text, leaving out repetitions where appropriate, simplifying the grammar, and omitting some clarifications that made their way into the full text. To give an example, in discussing the Italian soldier Gadda exclaims in parentheses: 'quali fatiche devo durare io per radunare i miei picconi e i miei badili!'; 'what hardships I have to endure to gather together my picks and shovels!' As this is something of an aside, it comes upon us quickly in the performance and we have: 'what hardships I have to endure!', which is lacking, yet maintains the self-pitying tone.

Having said this, we decided to keep all the lines from Shakespeare. This causes obvious problems in a number of places, the lines being either too long or having too short a time on the screen. However, we did not feel ourselves up to the task of editing the Bard and we recognised that such editing might even cause more confusion. In the end, trusting that the lines from *Hamlet* might even be well known enough for the audience to be familiar with them as they read them, we reproduced them in their entirety. We also had to deal with ad-libs: Gifuni's performance is energetic and even spontaneous, and his 'Turn off that mobile phone, you're in the trenches now' and theatrical repetitions were things that we sought to preserve and relay through the subtitles.

In considering the translation as a whole, we must conclude that we did our best, as Weaver recommended, and worked with care and intelligence within our limitations as scholars and translators. There may have been no perfect translation, but there are some renderings that pleased us immensely: Adolfo Trinchero, the commercial traveller 'che pronuncia Wagner all'italiana, come Agnese', instead 'pronounces Wagner as an Italian word, like lasagna'. I also enjoyed tackling the phrase 'Addio Gadda, e in gamba! neh! Mi saluti tanto suo fratello' by the Captain, whom we had the pleasure of transposing to a British member of the *hofficer* class circa 1916: 'Goodbye, Gadda, and Good Luck, what! Give my best to your brother'. The capitalisation is my favourite feature of that line, after the miraculous harmony between *neh* and *what*, and while such a small and, in fact, probably contentious detail seems a strange thing to find pride in, it shows to what extent this work lived in our heads. The characters, the different voices of the narrator – they felt real and we did our best by them. Where we have not rendered perfection there are only honest failures, and that is what is meant by doing one's best.

Endnote

Loyalty, function and being a good lover

We approached our translation of Gadda's texts – here cut up and spliced by the theatrical imagination of Fabrizio Gifuni – with a clear idea of our target audience, having been already familiar with the works in question. It is fair to say that the popularity of Gifuni's production in Italy also, to some extent, conditioned our thinking. Here was a chance to produce a translation informed by scholarship that could have a popular readership in the vast Anglophone system in addition to specialists from Gadda studies and Italianists in general. As Gifuni states in the Preface, he came to see these texts as central to any comprehension of the present-day conditions of Italy. In the same way, we saw that the resulting Gadda-Gifuni could speak to others today, a map not just of the 'chromosomes of Italy and the Italians', but of the whole of Europe, the West, the world perhaps.

With this in mind, we identified our target audience as a rather broad church of interested readers. We considered that they may have any number of academic disciplines behind them: Italianists, obviously, but also historians of the First World War, of fascism and politics, comparative literature scholars and theoreticians of the theatre. We also allowed that these would have sufficient interest in the topics and themes of the text – and we had to consider it as one text – and that they would not be put off by having occasionally to pick up a dictionary, encyclopaedia or mouse to check an obscure word or reference. However, we were conscious of not exhausting the reader's patience unduly, and we wanted the translation to be usable at all levels, from student work on the Great War and Italy under fascism to advanced research on Gadda's poetics, style and circulation. Finally, the target audience were not expected to be using this text for a performance in the way that Gifuni did. That is not to say that such a thing would be impossible, only that the translation might have turned out markedly different had we imagined that the text would be spoken aloud or recited.

With this in mind, we began our work. This was to be a functional translation, a translation that conformed to notions of translating as a purposeful activity and to the standard practice of translator invisibility, what the old-fashioned among us might call invisible faithfulness. In the first place, our work is indebted to Christiane Nord's *Translating as a Purposeful Activity* and her identification of the place in *Skopostheorie* for the relationship between the source-text author and the translator. Her thesis is that this relationship is one of *loyalty* above *faithfulness*:

> Let me call 'loyalty' this responsibility translators have towards their partners in translational interaction. Loyalty commits the translator bilaterally to the source and target sides. It must not be mixed up with fidelity or faithfulness, concepts that usually refer to a relationship holding between the source and the target *texts*. Loyalty is an interpersonal category referring to a social relationship between *people*. (Nord 1997: 125 – italics in the original)

Nord's idea is that the translator is in a position to decide how the intentions of an author are represented in a target text, and that this position posits a responsibility for the translator: hence *loyalty* to those intentions, superseding that of *faithfulness* to a text.

As I have said at the outset, the translators on this project are not new to Gadda, and therefore were in a good position to judge the author's intentions throughout the text. This meant that we were able to justify slight simplifications of Gadda's often torturous syntax in the name of loyalty, where a more faithful rendition would seem extreme, beyond acceptable, in English. This meant, in places, a simplification of punctuation, an increase in the number of sentences and, as we have seen above, the concretisation of some abstract concepts such as *la rinuncia*.

This approach naturally places strong emphasis on the interpretations that the translator makes. In our case, these did not always favour the *loyal* option, as can be seen from several moments in the translation, especially late on when the reader is confused by sentence structure, vocabulary and imagery. We felt here that the Italian text abandoned the readers to their confusion and so felt justified in replicating *faithfully* these features rather than helping them through with heavily interpreted shortcuts, simplifications or explanations. It would be stretching the concept of *loyalty* as espoused by Nord to argue that such a translation reflects Gadda's deep intentions and therefore counted as a *loyal* translation, but we are happy to say instead that our translation is at least *functional* in this respect.

A further word on invisibility. This is the default position of the Anglophone translator, and to some degree, it is the accepted standard expected by the Anglophone reader of translations, *pace* Venuti. The translator wishing to be read will do well to take this into account. The phrase that springs to mind is Jackson Mathew's remark, reported by veteran translator of Dante and Machiavelli as 'being a good lover' and 'being faithful without seeming to be' (Musa 1984: 63). Mathew's position as a very early entrant in the field of translation studies makes him a marginal and forgotten figure nowadays, but his insight is still of use to the modern practitioner. His opinions were sought along with Vladimir Nabokov's in Brower's *On Translation*, one of the earliest books to consider translation as a field of study in 1959. For our purposes, we may characterise his thesis – which in fact amounts to practical advice – as a kind of *positive invisibility*. The translator is expected to become as neutral a filter as possible for the reader of the target text to receive the source text. In truth, this is not a very sophisticated or very profound way of thinking about translation. As a piece of advice, it borders on the mendacious, because it posits the impossible position of complete neutrality, of complete equivalence. It is a difficult theory to swallow for the modern reader: but it does conform largely to our aims in our production of the current work. By this rather strange statement, we mean that once our motives, our agendas and our limitations have been acknowledged we can proceed with our invisibility in a way that will best reflect the value of the work as the author intended. To *being a good lover* we add Nord's *loyalty* and functionalism in order to produce the best translation that we can at any one time.

The last word, therefore, belongs not to the translator, or even the author, who are bound together now, for better or worse. Through our choices, we have put things that we have read and rewritten before a reader to make use of them or not as they choose. And this is the point of all translation and all interesting uses of space.

Staging

Giuseppe Episcopo and Federica G. Pedriali

L'ingegner Gadda va alla guerra is a story of furor and a story of ashes. It is also the account of the transition from furor to ashes. Set in apposition to the primary title *Eros e Priapo*, the parenthetic *Da furore a cenere* signals life's perversion – the biological continuum – right from the start. If we are looking for what unites Gadda's motifs, we can stop and look no further. It is here, in *Eros e Priapo*, in what can be considered his second anthropological treatise, that Gadda specifies the attribute of a concept in hendiadys – furor and ashes – whose earliest gestation appears already in his *Giornale di guerra*, running from then on like a karst river under all the works to come.

Human history and natural history. This is what for Gadda the continuum entails, in an all-inclusive non-theistic monotheism (Antonello 2003). There are kingdoms, classes, orders, families and genera; there is indeed the Linnaean taxonomy of the natural world. What the biological principle achieves is to make any accidental connections empirically discernible. We are part of that biological unity. The cycle of life fulfils its aim, the perpetuation of life (the transmissible line) against individual death, and it does so by entangling itself (*us*-itself) in one single chain. It is along this line that both logically and biologically the genus (the Aristotelian *universal*) subsumes the individual (the sensible *particular*). Similarly, and therefore grappling with logical and biological implications, human history is about the intertwining of not one but two dimensions, or layers, in a sort of synecdochal and counter-synecdochal network in which the part stands for the whole as much as the whole stands for its parts. The ascending-descending chain described, for instance, in *Meditazione milanese* exemplifies this, metonymically: 'Reality can be compared to a city: a city is made of houses, and the house is made of walls. And the wall is made of bricks: and the brick is made of particles' (MM SVP 752). On the side of identity this results in the subject becoming superfluous, endangered: 'the most recent physical, id est physico-mathematical, biophysical, psychological, psychiatric theories have joined forces against the idol-Ego, that tough piece of wood. They have destroyed, once and for all, the fetishist idea of a persisting, resisting, time-immanent Self' ('Come lavoro', 1949 – VM SGF I 428). The biological compass gets massively enlarged on such lines. It is in this way that Gadda ends up ascribing nature and culture to a zone that we could call of indifference (Benedetti 1995):

> An automatic telephone exchange; a radio station; a modern stage (complete with the most complicated mechanical, lighting, electrical devices): they aren't less natural than the sulphurous volcano, the barren banks of the stream, and the droppings of animals, whether four- or two-footed. Those products of human intelligence are indeed products: therefore they are natural, since the creative mind is natural, and the whole of human history is natural too. (MM SVP 876–7)

Everything is nature for Gadda: everything is interconnected, suspended in a state of equilibrium 'by polar tension' (VM SGF I 428). This is why he can view the multiplicity of the world of phenomena in its constitutive unity. Each object, matter, event – in sum the observable   is but the surface effect of its endomorphism, among traces of genetic memory and the expectation of its becoming, of its next state, and all of this engraved on its skin. Being suspended between past and future, the value of the observable for Gadda lies, then, in the categories of time and space, and corresponds to probability measures on these vectors, to which he adds the individual as vector (Pedriali 2007a: 176). He may appear to give Heisenberg's uncertainty principle epistemological implications. However, rather than to speculative metaphysics, such assumptions pertain to a heuristic method that is both organic and synthetic (Roscioni 1995a: 154), the kind of double helix that can result from two spirals, one biological, organic and genealogical, the other logical, inorganic and historical.

It is certainly not for the sake of epistemology that Gadda moves on from Spinoza, Leibniz and Kant to embrace the tensions surrounding hard science. Similarly, if we put these considerations forward, it is not for the sake of a theoretical premise. We want, rather, to enter the world of Gifuni's staging of Gadda as directly as possible, by stating, equally directly, how deeply rooted in Gadda's very apparatus this play is through the unleashing of what we will call the original naked furnace of language. Gadda's method of enquiry, to round off our non-premise, works as it must; it works, that is, as a brain-frame whose task it is to process sets of specimens. By deriving growing numbers of variables and applying them to such specimens, the brain-frame *Gadda* performs its task, getting to know its world through the endorsing-deforming of the available data sets. While struggling with the *unobservable* (the endomorphism of anything observable – object, matter or event), it altogether uplifts representation to a totally constructed level of baroque mimesis, with the resulting act externalised and placed *before* the subject – in sum, what we perceive as *reality*:

> To understand Gadda's baroque, one must keep in mind Gadda's stated premise that the universe is baroque, while rejecting the implication that his texts are that world's mimetic transcription. (Dombroski 1999: 18 – with reference to the much quoted line 'the Baroque and the Grotesque are already immanent in things', CdD RR I 760)

To these points of entry into the staging of Gadda we can now add the First World War. Freud's coeval theories eminently reflect the rapture, the new utter incommensurability of experience. Concepts such as repetition compulsion and death drive originated from exactly that context. And from there, from the specifics to which they were first applied, from the technical papers, for instance, officially reporting to the Austrian War Ministry the 'unconscious inclination in the soldier to withdraw from the demands, dangerous or outrageous to his feelings, made upon him by active service' (Freud 1955: 212), they did reverberate, far and wide, spreading the condition they were identifying and naming for the next two decades, through to the *next* carnage. Walter Benjamin for his part, in 1936, in his essay on Nikolai Leskov, famously connected the First World War and the trauma now endlessly weighing on the contemporary mind: 'For never has experience been contradicted more thoroughly than strategic experience by tactical warfare, economic experience by inflation, bodily experience by mechanical warfare, moral experience by those in power' (Benjamin 1968: 84). Italy was no exception – a case of collective trauma made actually all the more serious by additional specifics. The conflict that should have marked a further feat of resurgence, the country's latest war of independence, had in fact been mishandled. Worse, it had resulted in Caporetto and fascism, the events at the core of Gadda's *Giornale di guerra* and *Eros e Priapo*. Like Freud's compulsive soldier, like so many (the shell-shocked many) facing the *new and improved* universal condition, Gadda too noted and withdrew from service, while never declining to be serviceable, compulsively driven by the newly named death drive on behalf of the mishandled nation and calling Italy the chaos of the world, the accidental specimen in a natural history of destruction. Given what he shares, and with how much humankind, his paroxystic intellectual sharpness should not take us in.

What does it mean to gather all of this before us too in an instance of staging? *L'ingegner Gadda va alla guerra* marks the logistics where various scattered maledictions come together in stark mournful crescendo. The resonant wasteland of warfare faces us, through this, with its tonality initially set to minor, among echoes of the subject that never was and now is exponentially no more. The full range of military strategies gets mimicked via the vocal motions of which the named, like the accused – Amleto Pirobutirro, our Hamlet – is still capable while in dialogue with the absence of dialogue itself, with one's own other dead voices, against presages of action and final assaults that never come and yet scatter death in the trenches. War reveals itself in this suspended cruelty, shows how it pushes decay forward. All bodies get there – there is method in that madness too – pushed forward to the blast that will rip apart what cannot, what shouldn't be seen: the human order of things dying in the biological body. Hence the ashes, the second term in the hendiadys: but also the fury, the only state of mind we should come from. These two markers indicate the two end points orienting the progress of plurality as a chain of transformations (combination, coimplication, deformation, dissolution) and reducing outraged singularity – the living fury of the human domain – to totally spent matter. It is not enough, as Gadda understands only too well, to place before us the organic and the inorganic, the biological and the mineral, dynamis and energeia. The real killer is this inevitable, unsuppressable motion. The relentlessness of *L'ingegner Gadda va alla guerra* stages all this to perfection.

It is true and it has been noted. Despite its documentary intent (Bonifacino 2011; Cenati 2011), *Giornale di guerra* records few images of dead bodies (Mileschi 2007; Carta 2010). Staging the text brings this peculiarity into further evidence, showing how already at source, even before becoming Amleto Pirobutirro, the diligent incinerated soldier establishes a first distance, a fundamental difference between death and dying. The miserable and humiliating monotony of war circulates as destructive progress, in the crescendo of the play, right from the beginning in minor, affecting first the body, then spreading as numbness of the mind, then permeating, possessing the psyche to the point when war starts to haunt the soldier's nights: 'A restless night and sad dreams: perhaps the first war dream I have ever had.' From the moment when this dying of body and mind is cognised as fully enforced – registered and noted – the subject eagerly awaits its purest and most brutal, its most destructive manifestation: death extended to one's other, to one's only real life; the death of one's closest, Enrico's death. This death that would be one's own because it couldn't be that of an unknown, unmarked dead soldier, is the thought, the hypothesis that cannot be stated and yet gets constructed through the vow that the brother be spared. The inexpressible is what sustains the relapses, what supports the desire to restore a pre-war state of indolence, when indolence was not yet fury fully understood: when the drive to reduce life to a merely conservative organic condition had been only just fathomed. It is only in the very last segment of the *Giornale*, when the news of that death has been broken and there is no more disguising or concealing, no more postponing or sparing oneself the evidence of one's ultimate dying mental content, that Gadda finally admits his automatic state ('My life is useless. It is that of an automaton survivor of himself'). He still fails to see, however, that despite being indolently death-driven and hence purely organic ('I will end my troubled life in the old swamp of indolence') the recording and the noting, for him at least, are not over yet, statements to the contrary notwithstanding ('I will no longer write anything down').

Staging this Gadda brings forth this Hamlet, the doppelgänger redoubled in a minimum of at least two souls, kept alive by an unvanishing death wish. Not classifiable as a survivor, our hero belongs to the undead. He is a biological body conveying its organic subjectivity, exhibiting the organic life of man as subject (echoes of Deleuze are slipping in here). He is someone whom the blast furnace has transformed further than death ever will, leaving behind incombustible hybrid residue: cinders that are neither soma (flesh, blood) nor sarx (butchered livestock, meat, corpse). A face stripped of the face, exactly as in a painting by Francis Bacon (definitely Deleuze is coming in handy) – naked biology that has moved to the foreground:

> The body is the Figure, or rather the material of the Figure. Above all the material of the Figure is not to be confused with the material structure in space which is separate from this. The body is a Figure, not structure. Conversely, the Figure being a body, is not a face and does not even have a face. It has a head, because the head is an integral part of the body. It can even be reduced to its head. There is a big difference between the two. For the face is a structured spatial organisation which covers the head, while the head is an adjunct of the body, even though it is its top. (Deleuze 2003: 15)

Gadda too unwraps, reveals the *head*, represents not the dead but the dying body – the endomorphism beneath, the pulsating material of the Figure: 'For me facts, objects, events count in as much as they make us expectant of what will be next, or recall what preceded and caused them' ('Un'opinione sul neorealismo', 1951 – VM SGF I 629). This unmaking is indeed an execution – not just a representation. It is the ultimate war machinery by subject, text and stage, in response to the provocation mounted by the all too dear catastrophe.

To be absolutely unequivocal. What we have called execution is only up to a point an execution (of a score or a script). Of course, *L'ingegner Gadda va alla guerra* is an extraordinary feat of textual orchestration and staging (an execution). Fascism, for instance, gets scripted as the resist-ible centre of disequilibrium. It is, more precisely, the centre reversibly adjustable to either temporal ends of a bipartite performative sequence taking us from the First World War to the Second. At no moment, in this score, can one avoid picking fascism as the ticklish subject and the ticklish melodic line of the day – including our day, which by the way is the day of the nation's celebrations just past (2011: Italy's 150th since Unification). Gadda here faces up to the political specifics of the anthro-pological problem stated at source: 'Italians are happy when they can persuade themselves that they have done something while in reality they have done no such thing.' This sentence, in Gifuni's inexhaustible mental acrobatics, has mathematical commutative properties and invites the reversal of its operands, thus becoming as true as its contrary: Italians are happy when they can persuade themselves of not having committed what they actually did commit. *L'ingegner Gadda va alla guerra* is keen to orchestrate all of this, even by implication, while also suggesting the execution, yes, of a vast modern epic, right from the start, right from the first universalising adagio: 'Life is without season, without joy.'

But then there is another execution. The incombustible residue left behind by an exhausted *Giornale* suddenly ignites again. The language turns violent, explicit, graphic: consciously and deliberately grim, brutal, sarcastic. Under attack from an energy excess that could know no end, we cross over to where a different time, that of *Eros e Priapo*, is *same time*. The 'Homeland of delirium' has merely unfolded-carnivalised further, and now Eros truly reigns through a Mussolini invested with omnivorous sexual appetite and acting as the Phallus, as the one and only engine of History: 'He was the prime mover, he was the first and autochthonous force and the glorious impulse that set the entire machine in motion.' His masculinity is not just exhibited, inflationary and insane.

It leaves no room, it penetrates all. The two genders couldn't be more suited to stress the totality of the action by the Leader: 'All that rubbing and creaking and panting and sweating, were all thanks to the Doosh-y: to the Great Khan!' Everything becomes an extension of his body: 'The Doosh-y, the homeland and the Ethiopian Empire, hibiscus tea, the rods of the lictors, the projecting cannons of the Littorio were forever incarnate, consubstantial and welded together in the projection of the pizzle of the Life-Bringer.' And all this to embed one's own image into the dying matter of a nation possessed by her defeats, by her deadly hope to have 'sons, sons, sons' ('in litters of eight like rabbits') – an infinite number of sons to 'send to war, war, war'. As Deleuze and Guattari have pointed out, so rightly: 'There is fascism when a war machine is installed in each hole, in every niche' (Deleuze and Guattari 1987: 236). Few lines could be closer to this Gadda.

Or perhaps not. There will always be lines that can hit close to the heart of the matter, even if there is no such organ left in the body of the soldier that once was. Gifuni, for his part, has lent his entire body-mind to this mounting capital execution of yesterday's and today's Italy: to a literature of imputation claiming that trauma can certify truth over and above the divide of autobiography and historiography, since both can assume the perspective of the End. Theatre and theatre training clearly have their advantages over most other forms of exegesis and critical thinking. In compressing its sources into this new Gadda, this performative capital execution of One's Times gives us one entirely spent set of *res gestae* by the unknown soldier left behind by the natural history of Service – what could be called, given the practical solutions adopted, a Brechtian strategy of cunning. Amleto Pirobutirro comes on stage to tell a story which is placed at an organic distance for him and does not coincide with either the intertext (*Hamlet*) or the original framework (*Giornale di guerra* and *Eros e Priapo*). Rather than a displacement technique, this new story is his way to tell the truth through further multiple punitive lacerations – a kind of *ulciscetur iniurias hostium*. 'We gain our knowledge of life in a catastrophic form' (Brecht 2004: 94). Again, few lines could be closer to Gadda, but this we have already said. Crime novels, this is what matters, because this is what Brecht had in mind when writing those lines, let readers face the catastrophe. Gifuni, by plunging this *oeuvre au noir* into the matrix of history, has had no hesitations in this regard – no qualms, no squeamishness. Gadda knows (oh, how he knew) that murder is his poetics, world-making extracted from that awful mess.

Endnote

Gadda cultivated his writing *plus* – including performative writing destined for technologies other than the book – in the age of mechanical reproduction. Applying to him the notion of the author as producer may be taking things too far, but thanks to his job at the RAI (Ungarelli 1993a), in the 1950s Gadda was someone actively involved in the newest forms of mass communication. Between 1952 and 1958 Radio RAI Terzo programma broadcast various of his radio works, including one series (1952: *I quattro Luigi*, but only three King Louis of France were realised in the end – *I Luigi di Francia*, LdF SGF II 85–211), one translation (1954: *La verità sospetta*, VS SVP 297–378, from Juan Ruiz de Alarcón y Mendoza's play *La verdad sospechosa*), one adaptation (1955: *Un radiodramma per modo di dire. Háry János*, SS SVP 1037–91; the source for the dialogue was the libretto of Zoltán Kodály's 1926 *Liederspiel* based on a poem by János Garay), and a further original dialogue for three voices (1958: *Il guerriero, l'amazzone, lo spirito della poesia nel verso immortale del Foscolo*, GASP SGF II 375–429). Off the air he was also more than ready to give normative advice on matters of writing for the radio (1953: *Norme per la redazione di un testo radiofonico* – SGF I 1081–91).

Writing for the cinema also tempted him somewhat and more than once. The short story 'Accoppiamenti giudiziosi' (1957 – AG RR II 891–920), in particular, had in his view the potential to become a film script – or, anyway, Gadda toyed with the idea long enough to leave traces behind, and these have recently resurfaced (Gadda 2011: 471–9). Already a few years earlier, in the late 1940s, the collapse of *Quer pasticciaccio*, his most novelistic project, had resulted in a fully scripted screenplay (*Il palazzo degli ori*, 1947–8, published posthumously in 1983, PdO SVP 925–87). On that earlier occasion Gadda had appeared 'to be ready to exchange textual complexity for visual popularity, the old medium for the new one'. Yet, in doing so, he had not only confirmed 'his interest in more popular forms of expression' but also allowed his most persistent obsessions to be organised by a medium which could be employed 'to reel out frame after frame of subconscious material' (Pedriali 2007b – for insights into the structure of the treatment, see also Santi 2008). The script of *Il palazzo degli ori* may have come to nothing, but *Pasticciaccio* in turn was adapted first for the big screen, then for television. In the first instance – *Un maledetto imbroglio* (1959), directed by Pietro Germi – the story gets set in the 1950s, close to the director's concerns, and hence, perhaps not inappropriately, to the neorealist climate of the novel's year of publication (Gutkowski 2002); Gadda apparently did appreciate the film. With the 1983 television adaptation in four episodes by Piero Schivazzappa, the laws of the TV drama instead erase partly the linguistic *pastiche*, partly the narrative eccentricity and especially the lack of cathartic ending of the original. Both adaptations are characterised, in short and not surprisingly, by major departures from the book.

The theatre marks an altogether different success story in this writing *plus*. With minor exceptions, Gadda did not write for the stage; perhaps he too saw it as platform under threat from the newer technologies, from cinema primarily. And yet starting from the first production of his *Gonnella buffone*, a play based on a sixteenth-century novella by Matteo Bandello (1953 – GB SVP 989–1036), his texts, destined as they were for the life of printed matter, have been produced with increasing frequency, and in many performance formats. For a selective listing to 2001, see Longhi (2001b). Luca Ronconi's theatre edition of *Pasticciaccio* (1996: Teatro Argentina, Rome; then 1997, for stage and television, in collaboration with Giuseppe Bertolucci) marks the key development in this sense. 'Luca Ronconi was the first visual interpreter to openly engage with *Quer pasticciaccio* in its integrity', resulting in the characters being deprived of psychological life and playing the pure 'bearers of Gadda's voice', literally, word by word (Marchesini 2007). It was a stunning theatre experience – one that proved, almost above all, the phenomenal aural power of this literature. Performances, plays, recitals, readings, new theatrical pieces based on or inspired by had to follow. Among them (and the listing gets ultra-selective here): Fabrizio Gifuni's 'L'incendio di via Keplero' (2005: Rome Auditorium; with soundscape support by cellist Mario Brunello); Raimondo Morelli's *Quer pasticciaccio* (2007: Teatro Le Salette, Rome); Simonetta Pusceddu's ballet *Partitura per minestrone. Balletto in un solo atto* (2010: Teatro Massimo, Cagliari); Lorenzo Loris' *L'Adalgisa* (2011, 2012: Teatro Out Off, Milan); Paolo Bessegatto's 'L'incendio di via Keplero' (2011: Teatro Sociale, Bergamo); Lorenzo Montanini's play for an audience of fifteen people, *Un pasticciaccio* (2011: Teatro Studio Uno, Rome). *Eros e Priapo*, in particular, has been the real discovery. Luca Scarlini and Massimo Verdastro's take on the text (under the direction of Roberto Bacci) toured the country from 2004 to early 2012, including performances at the prestigious Teatro Valle in Rome; Adriana Martino's has had two full seasons since 2010. In the last decade, Milan in particular, as Gadda's home city, has seen a real flourishing of activities, starting from *Gadda e Milano* (2001), a medley of primary texts created and directed by Claudio Beccari for the Teatro dei Filodrammatici. The latest initiative, Giuseppina Carutti's *A Milano con Carlo Emilio Gadda* (2011–13), combines exhibitions (*Le carte di Gadda alla Trivulziana*, Archivio Storico Civico and Biblioteca Trivulziana), seminars, performances and readings by established Gadda actors (among others Fabrizio Gifuni, Anna Nogara, Franca Nuti and Massimo Popolizio). In May 2012, as part of this rich programme, Fabrizio Gifuni presented his latest performance-homage *Gadda e il teatro, un atto sacrale di conoscenza. Letture, congetture, notazioni su un amore mai totalmente espresso* (Laboratorio Fantoli, Politecnico di Milano); his audio-book '*Quer pasticciaccio brutto de via Merulana*' – *letto da Fabrizio Gifuni* came out in October 2012. This is to say, in short, given that lists have got to be both finite and conclusive, that the success of *L'ingegner Gadda va alla guerra*, its 121 performances in Italy in two seasons plus first forays *extra muros* in Russia and the UK between 2011 and 2012, is far from being isolated. Just like King Wenceslas, in Alfred Jarry's *Ubu Roi*, Gadda is very much alive and has many grandsons.

World-making

Federica G. Pedriali

Each fact or act of this world is finite however much we may wish it not to be the case.

Carlo Emilio Gadda

No, not the sunshine

Let me digress straight away. Gadda is not exactly the sunshine of reading. Too gluey and self-saturating. Yet this sticky substance captures the Italian language like no other. There is no risk of exaggerating here. Forget most of the canon. Even the top names could learn a trick or two from this guy.

Expert readers have developed expert methods to deal with the challenge. One sure way to make Gadda work is to turn the tables for the Gadda that doesn't work. Take his plots. Things (words) get so trapped in them that it is hard to tell even whether the line is taut or sagging. Is this plot? digression? malfunction? genius?

Everything sticks in these fictions, gets nowhere and everywhere in one, blessed and cursed at the same time for hampering and realising the author's vision, his duplicitous double intention to achieve both control and loss of control. Pity, in a sense, that Gadda has got the stamina to attempt both accounts of the world – the all and the all of the mind. Through sheer hubris he does get there somehow. The problem is that we don't, that there is no way we can keep up with his level of scrutiny into the puzzle of matter. Yes, Gadda is at best very tough sunshine; reader feedback is absolutely unanimous on this. And yet, on this most definite of difficulties we also do get our chance. Gadda, we can argue, is terribly good for theory. Any theory.

Oily standards

Let me digress again. It is bad news even without Gadda. The universe stinks, and my part in it, which is the part of the average subjectivity, is to make sure that no one notices. I classify, organise, summarise. I exist in order to commit my perceptual system to value judgments. There is advantage, gratification almost, in cognising this set in opposition to that set, in siding with the mode of cognition that wins me not just the task but also the power to conduct tasks in general. There is, above all, the conviction that, because I have got method and (perhaps) even reason on my side, I obtain results; better still, I obtain stable results, both in here and out there, the latter being where I locate all that requires my thrust forward, call it my anthropological need to appropriate, in order to master.

I surely participate. I accept, that is, the laws and the customs of participation. I make myself useful, contribute to the collective effort; I collectively reinforce the rule that is nonetheless set. I get cognised, marked, indeed fully participated in turn, even before the exercise becomes collective practice. I certainly get picked or not picked at disjunctions, for I am invariably either their leading or their lesser member. And yet, although my participation is no more than a participation in polarities, I cannot withdraw my support from the venture, not even when I get excluded, discarded, assigned to the lesser regions, spent to my personal disadvantage.

In this way, and it is no small paradox, I end up doing equal work in either camp. One superior outcome (supra-individual reason), one world (one uni-verse), one cohesive action (one gluey discourse) must result, in fact, from my agency as subject, regardless of whether the overall package stems, in my respect, primarily from an allocation to this or that side of the divide. The ultimate agent – cognitive imprint – is not at all bothered by my personal details; my personal binary (dis)comfort fits, actually, quite nicely in the larger scheme of things. The fitting even goes as far as giving me, in my allocation, the complementary conviction that, since there is now my imperfection, there must have once been original perfection. Moreover, I do not just prove the past, the corruption of the origin, with my subjectivity. With it, I also point to the future, my stronger, my pulling pole. There, in the future, I will not simply rejoin the origin (this would be good, but still it wouldn't be good enough). There I will surpass the origin altogether, having come from feats of perfective action, individually and collectively. At least this is the plan. The good old All re-perfected and improved, after a long history of deterioration coinciding with *me*. Otherwise, what would be the reason for us to hang around in the schema? Definitely quite neat, as persuasions go.

This is it then. Digress further or differently as we may, our cognitive architecture imposes acceptance on us. Convenience all round – highest assimilation rate guaranteed. The narrative works, backed up by the principle governing it. What could be better, indeed, than this best of all worlds? Rome 1927. Two crimes. A burglary and a murder – a real mess. A woman is the victim in both cases, but only the second crime leaves no decency unturned. As governed narrative, as gendered mental content, this best of worlds is horrendously comfortable, shocking and straightforward in equal measure, although figuring it out, especially on paper, gets one terribly embroiled. For what is one up to, really, in this glue? A murdered woman. A woman so badly murdered that you have to assume that she deserved it (it is always practical, when life couldn't get any stickier, to digress into the most dialogic form of address and deal with the you in you as *you*). The messiest crime, or rather the awful *it* of matter – but not before you are done with it as gender, the opposite gender.

Gadda comes in on such cues. The cosmic routine spares no one; undoubtedly, it did not spare him. This is why he must expose the universal mishap. He has understood the plot; he must find ways to make others understand it too. The immemorial concoction, the pre-established narrative that gets going each time, each time never any less stale than on day one, is here for the taking, and can be broken down into parts, a small cast of parts – she, you, we, one, I. There they go. Object of desire (*she*). Participant interlocutor (*you*). Collective plurality (*we*). Singular plurality as pure genus (*one*), the pure genus (pure species) standing in the way of the subject: namely and quite narrowly, the (un)generic, (in)definite antagonist to the guy who gets most embroiled of all, and most of the times declaredly so (*I*). It sounds complicated but actually isn't, all duly activated, broken down, extricated from the mix in parts and in turns, because in matter matters are not just inextricable. For us at least, totality comes arranged in strings, clusters, patterns, series, sets, names, facts, people.

Causes. Above all causes and causal links. The critical spin that Gadda gives to such basics is phenomenal. By his lights, causes ultimately are the task pushing on the happy gang, keeping it on track. We, indeed plurally, are the mindful partner. Or rather, we must mind those connections in earnest, even forcing them if necessary (it is always necessary). In a sense (the sense in which we decide to understand such things), the universe reserves its very best dynamism to us, so that together we gain (a bit of a motto, this one, but the general stickiness gets well oiled in this way). Grease (grease, fats, oils are marked vocab in Gadda's lexicon), the kind of grease that comes from rubbing matter with mind (the two having first been separated for our mental convenience) does manage to turn a potentially inert mass in need of activation (Gadda's famously gluey dumplings, say) into a fine piece of machinery reassuringly producing the motions of the regulated life (whatever it is that goes under this caption). Such are the advantages of this arrangement that its terms and conditions are worth advertising over and over again, even here. Acceptance is all that it takes. No more no less. Minimum effort, for maximum results. Gadda couldn't be more serious, or more satirical, in this regard. For once, and despite the many statements to the contrary, his inner divisions are perfectly balanced. A smooth downward gliding through the Ages of Man. He laughs, he laughs wildly at the comfortable cognitive ride which should have been his, by default, and instead was missed through wanting it too badly.

These being the broad principles, there is scope, plenty, for digressing even more substantially – relentlessly if you like. Gadda very much likes that, digressing mercilessly into the plot, nothing but the plot. But what about us? When reading Gadda we are fully mindful, on red alert in actual fact. Sagging, taut, parenthetic. Dialogic, obsessive, primary, ancillary. Busying itself with theory (any theory). Mixing theory with detail (any detail, as all detail is fiendish). We note as expected. We observe, that is, how Gadda's thought works. We do well, amazingly well for a while. We love it. He is the greatest of them all, our hero without a doubt. Then, suddenly, we give it up altogether, semantically, syntactically, morphologically bruised by the hubristic excess of this line of attack on life, only too happy to go back to managing it again broadly and generally, as broadly and as generally as contractually possible (a contract is always there, in human affairs, however immaterial the commerce).

For instance, in *Quer pasticciaccio*, what did you make of that downright oddity, Inspector Ingravallo, Gadda's alter ego, going out to check the industrial formula for personal existential success? The two crimes that were excellent, in Rome 1927, burglary and murder, one grotesque, one hideous, are behind us by this stage, and we are beginning to grudge exactly that. Ingravallo has been shuffling paperwork in his mental office for several pages, and this cognitive admin, a sort of clearing of the binary desk, instead of clarifying the part played by his data in the making of the Mess, is quickly draining the system's charge. Enough is enough, and indeed, as if this wasn't bad enough, with the closure of chapter three in sight, the text gleefully embarks on a further lateral sub-unit, a technical mini-mission in the form of a police visit to the local branch of the Standard Oil. Oil as in transformer oil, of all businesses. Riveting stuff.

But wait. The rival, the subject's allergen (if you allow) works there (if you can call winning clients work). The sexual innuendo (because clients, like women, must be pursued, wooed to the last, made to fall for you, to establish the product's inimitable prowess) is not just one of life's bad jokes leading you on for a while if you are male, inspector and strictly single (strictly sexually rejected). In a world (in a fiction) in which we have swiftly moved from binary unease (the inspector's, primarily, at his own exclusion from life's proceedings, chapter one, incipit and lunch scene) to binary retribution (the horrific body on the floor, in the same apartment, after the coded warning of the burglary in the flat next door, chapters one and two), what is really emerging, in this roundabout way, is that there is no alternative message, no variation on the theme – no aside (no digression, no protection) from the general Mess. Standards are standards, very definitely and quite crucially for mankind's industry, with its greasy mechanics (reproduction) and dirty selling campaigns (essentially, value politics, the kind of VAT universally imposed at source through unconfessed parental (s)election and bringing about the preference for the better, the more gratifying continuator of *me*).

Every oil to its standards. Gadda certainly dares here. This oil business may be a clue to universal matters, and it may even be a clue to the entire textual network of the *Mess*, but it is enough to lose readers in droves. We have waited, still we are not riveted. Industrial reliability, reliability of the requisites that is – we do get it – must come first, always first (in the text it comes twice, both times marked, unusually, though reportedly, through the use of the italics). Reliability is the ultimate asset (quite rightly, in taking it satirically, a translator gets seriously excited at this point and gives out the *splendid firmness of the requisites* which not even Gadda, for all his daring, had really made explicit). Champions (champion oils) cannot, mustn't be resisted (do not resist it indeed, but do work out the concept for yourself: a standard champion, a champion in standards, someone, some top stallion, granted top performance in all standards: can anyone get any more standard than this?). To be utterly unequivocal, Gadda dares equivocally – let's concede as much. After all, he is the model equivocal citizen of the regime (any regime, be under no illusion: the Regime, the Management, got here long ago with the sad intention to stay). He is both intolerant of regimes (health, diet, work, relations, publishing houses, fascism, to name just a few relevant sources of bother) and perfectly regimented (the law, the army, the workplace, even the agon, the fascist agon that is, the most universal latest fad till it lasted, nearly get the best out this man, and if this isn't entirely the case, it is mostly *their* fault, as he laments with furious method).

Relentless. One could call it, and it would be correct, relentless mimesis. By Gadda's own admission, in fact, all that he does (though he does it baroquely) is to portray the Mess out there, picked and packaged as collective discourse ready for noting within the logistics of division. Viscosity, acidity, platonic love, cats in heat, resurrection, the Gospels, those who love me, the nail, the nail of truth . . . In the end, not even Ingravallo, the spokesman for the job, can take it any longer. Substance, properties, permanence – the venerable content of high discourse, the highest kind – get stripped, broken down, milled to a monstrous mixture of no substance whatsoever yet hammering home the one and only nail of truth, the single villainous plot. Rome the *caput mundi*, under the outrageous Regime. A murdered woman at the centre of this centre: where she stood symbolically, emphatically, for the Host, for Life itself. Damn cheat, in a damn fiction. Gadda is talking pure binarism here, in his Roman thriller, as elsewhere, packed as he himself is with corrupt universal content, oozing crap mimesis and crap standards. However, if this is really it, if the *uni*-verse can be in no way re-*versed* and this glue is the utter best we can ever hope to achieve, then there must be diabolical intent, not just talent to spare, in the subject's response to the general binary triumph.

Roughly we get it. His rival works for the local Standard. But Gadda cannot stop at the rough measure. Even broken down and fine-milled the plot gives away nothing but plot. Not by chance, then, Gadda grinds his message more finely still. This is what his relentlessness is all about, in an unrestrainable thought experiment which takes him to the notion of the minimal thinking body, the smallest mind unit conceivable – Leibniz's *petites perceptions*, say, one of Gadda's declared frames of reference. There, in a theory of the infinitely small, he still comes up against the laws and the practices of the Regime. The mechanism forging the standard; the standard bearing its *protégés*; those elected and guaranteed evolving forward, progressing and rising forth, at each new junction – however small and subliminal the junction. Again, we roughly follow this evolutionary wisdom irreversibly forging and rising word by word, line by line to the accepted (unacceptable) and advertised order of things. Yet its sustained application in radical degrees of linguistic fineness and satirical exposure does leave us stranded in textual micro-saturation, without much hope of dissolution into infinite reader regress. Indeed – if only we could slip into some infinity or other. At most, instead, we disengage from this level of cohesion, opt for the humane exit, open up gaps of resilience, non-reading, tangential misunderstanding, ultimately always going back to the broad and the rough, because, surprisingly, there appears to be room for manoeuvre in those. Somewhat paradoxically, it is at such awkward moments, when we skip it, drop it, try to get it out of our system, lose it momentarily or for good, that Gadda binds us most strongly, making our disengagement compossible with the impossible, in the perfect double-bind that comes from the toughest realisation in the repertoire: possibility and freedom being but a semblance breaking up (*gapping*) necessity, the opposite semblance.

Parallel gluten

Let me not stop digressing. World-making, model-making, checking on worlds already made – handling plot, in sum, is key. We do want story, happy ending. We want, above all, to postpone the end. Gadda exploits such basics, as he must. The needs are simple, yes – and contradictory. Surely, we need to be able to handle not just life but clearance, space-making, scale. Mental content casts its bulk about, requires breathing space; even if it didn't breathe, we do. Lined-up, especially lined-up on a page, it tangibly shows that, like every other solid, it too is gappy matter, in a gappy space of our construct, implemented and maintained in the agreed orders of magnitude and simplification (go below those, and it is you who is gone, gone below our universe, back to the preliminary clutter and babble, lost to useful human commerce).

Simple, integrative – a positive polarity story. Gadda would have loved to handle life for real. Even his negative assignment, the substitution he gets instead, can and must be made good. He can be useful still. He will reveal all, no less – it is his duty to achieve that at least. Many apologies, of course, if the happy ending must be revised, if postponing death is no longer really negotiable (very, very sorry). The plan is crystal clear right from the first drafts, at each new draft, and despite the increasing number of attempts. Pattern must be established with abbreviated urgency (*asap*). Gadda has got to synthesise origin (the original scene) and the cast (the core dramatis personae arranged around the core needs). With scale in place (a reduced mankind pitched in action against the incommensurable), he will extract both a first-level narrative (a unique series of event, the plot as such) and an extended connectivity (networked time and space: chains of human generations and relations). A big picture all right. The exemplary picture of the narratable and its pull. And all of it resulting, at the other end, in a plot exhausted, a narrative delivered, a revelation revealed. Obviously, a big picture is not the entire picture. Gadda understands this well: only the entire picture could do the entire job, in an entire account of causality. However, as entirety was never a given, never part of the cognitive remit, this size and scale of things could still do the trick – a trick taking in all involved, why not.

But one thing is the theory, the perfect legitimacy of one's response. Another, the practice: the actual perfecting. Gadda, for one, is seldom credited with perfecting much. Yet this particular deficiency, if it is a deficiency, doesn't play the negative matter of fact in his case. Forget Gadda's flair for textual saturation (cognitive gap filling through linguistic trituration). It is his imperfection we treasure: the big picture getting progressively aborted as the fast early drafting subsides into mounting early exhaustion (of the material, never of the author). After all, the grand narrative is nothing but banal (don't forget, it is nothing but plot), whereas its dispersal is all but uninteresting. The big oily motion, in fact, is not just generically resilient, and is not just feeding into other big pictures (other works) as the recyclable stuff of life and literature. Put aside increasingly for good, often literally consigned to the deepest trunk, the oil, the glue, the big story, the story of the world compacted down to an origin, a small primary cast, a pervasive biological plot and a binary totalitarian space-time, won't refrain from carrying on its work somehow, even though it appears to have been officially withdrawn. Once installed, the work works in you (Gadda's poetics in a tag). The work, or rather the novel, for it must be a novel, a large plot or little else, does work, that is, from within its own discontinuities. Above all, it works in the fruitful silent gap of the non-work (another authorial tag), till it finally returns from that non-life to prod you (haunt you) into action again (a standard enough descriptor, this one, if Gadda didn't get seriously spooked in the process). Hence, the renewed effort, the no effort spared, the case reopening and the pull returning for those aborted, not so aborted, in the end (im)perfectly realised big pictures. Forty years since Gadda's death, we are still gratefully sifting through the maddeningly rich debris. Whichever tag gets appended to it, whether authorially or by us, there is no lack of basic contradiction in this imperfection. The masterpieces, no doubt, contradict it. They are, and they are not few, what remains of the perfective effort to do away with storytelling altogether while doing nothing but telling the big story through the imperfect gappy/non-gappy item, the overloaded picture, the excess achievement, the loss of control partly reclaimed as control, partly left visibly unmended.

In a sense, again the broadest and roughest one possible, this is our Gadda – the Gadda we can best work with. Someone outraged by life but not so cankerous not to let us go. The difficulty, the relentlessness, the concentration, the pulverisation, the deflation, all the things which cannot be taken out because they make the equation, thus become the primary movers of an unmarked meta-textual exchange with the reader, a dialogue needing no intradiegetic cue to get going. Too much closure? Do feel free to dissent (use my work to do so). Not enough closure? Follow my tricks (exploit my tricks to delimit your world). Is there too much Eros in the system, despite an unloving, unerotic rule? Be my guests (be involved as far and as much as you can take *it* or *me*). (Can't take much? Enjoy at least my mental brackets, trusted markers of a divided thought.) This Gadda (our Gadda) is indeed a maddeningly rich scenario where one rests roughly assured that our author has used all the tricks in the book to perfect an imperfect cancellation of the evidence of his progress. The story sticks, the universe stinks, the subject sucks – so what. By the time Gadda asks, roughly rhetorically, 'Which action shall it be? Where shall I start from?', and then promptly answers, roughly poetically, 'But my actions are already in place, I have started already' (rough translation of the untranslated *Meditazione milanese*, opening lines – MM SVP 627), by then we are so forgetful, so possessed and energised (so maddened) by our late discovery of this key of keys to twentieth-century Italian thought that we take to it as if we had been granted our greatest wish, broadly and roughly. Room for manoeuvre guaranteed. Saturation, linguistic reification made safe, harmless. No end to rough reading (no end to our kind of knowledge). The mind feels too full? Too full exactly of what? And although too full and casting itself in a vote at each and every step, it won't affect its own trajectory, it won't manage to? Then, why exactly should we feel any obligation to provide the universe with a willing workforce? Yes, why consider ourselves indebted and morally bound – to the Glue?

Binarism is left untouched by Gadda. The order of things remains strictly singular under his management. The wild laughter dies out revolving vertiginously on itself, with no alternative or alternative companion but the awareness of its own potential for entrapment. And yet through Gadda we learn a lot that is plural and even parallel – a kind of parallel gluten, another compossible, and resulting from overloading, stuffing beyond capacity, passing through a minimum of two minds, which also gives a maximum of two texts, per text, the collapsed and the resurrecting, the bracketed and the non bracketed. The double matter of the mind pushes, presses for either outcomes, to make content collapse further, yield further and then further still, because two of everything was life's best ratio and law, and our subject, in attempting to expose the one Uncountable which indifferently calls him to account, is appealing precisely to that law. Having said this, however, we are again back full circle to the singular and the linear, which is where Gadda also fully belongs.

Line pull

Let me try to stop digressing. Taking exception, in the beginning, to *Tristram Shandy*, 1.22 ('Digressions, incontestably, are the sunshine') has led me to having just enough line left to bring in *Hamlet*, II, ii, 256–8. Does Gadda digress? Of course he does. Digression is a function of the plot, and plot is a function of the activation of the world. Does digression bring variety, maintain movement, buy us some freedom (some gaps) in his case too? On the surface of things of course it does. But ask me the question a second time, and the answer will be no, because Gadda, like Hamlet, knows how deep his conditionals can reach and how barely visible (imperfectly erased) the pull of his narrative line will be as a result – barely visible, that is, had he not had bad dreams. Similarly finite ('bounded in a nut shell') and yet counting himself unlimited ('a king of infinite space' – this is *Hamlet* still), Gadda has had indeed bad dreams. Not for a moment, in fact, does he lose the plot. Not even when he may have lost his text.

Arguably, the banality immediately achieved by Gadda in the drafts at the plot level predetermines (compromises) all later remedial attempts to expose the Grand Plot. Counter-arguably, in a compositional mess very much risking to run out of control, the other Gadda, the one working laterally in the nether regions of his workshop, has been busy scanning both old rejects and rejects-to-be looking for ways, all of them relentless, to turn first level banality (frustratingly not yet stinking of universals) into Superior Banality, the ultimate Stuff (Banality without banality – salvaged, redeployed and exhibited through a figurative minimum which is also the structural maximum allowed). The evidence we have (but we respond to it as if we didn't have it, for we readers and critics don't do dreams, especially not bad dreams about our Gadda) is that the various drafts break up along very comparable fault lines (not at all surprising, this, given that the whole mishap is the fault of systematic impersonal agents, the System for short), and that the subsequent re-work, combined with the non-work and the lateral cross-work, gets them massively but not drastically overhauled, maintaining and highlighting (imperfectly erasing, once again) exactly and especially those fault lines.

For our part, we continue not to do bad dreams. This is clearly the way we have shaped up collectively as Gadda readers and scholars. We even try not to do Cartesian space any more – too unambiguous and unique, too safely determined between its axes. Some of us, more daring than the rest, actually push those two inseparables, plot and digression, to the point where there are only digressions and no plot – no centre(s), yes, from which Gadda could stray (Dombroski 1999: 7), the perfect Deleuzian rhizome, the best incontestable disruption and variety of them all. Deployed by the text as we are at some level, and overcorrecting it theoretically in other respects, we would have indeed delighted and scared our author; for once he might even have counted himself lucky, whatever else it was that he counted himself in life – nutshell, king, infinite, bounded, desperate. However, counting oneself against the Uncountable through the services of the reader, in response to her response as it were, is undoubtedly still not it, and is still not enough – not with Gadda's style of pervasive authorship. A wakeful state of self-possession gives him the sense – not rough and not broad, on the contrary quite precisely pinpointable – that his reasons for exposing (*executing*) the overall insignificance are utterly *right* (i.e. procedurally *lawful*, as well as creatively *resourceful*), as they are private and shameful. Once again, Hamlet's case.

Attempted several times and finally realised through a mix of original drafts and extraneous material, Gadda's third major narrative, *L'Adalgisa* (1944), is one such instantiation of a plot discontinued, reselected, redeployed, saturated and sealed. Most readers declare it lost to digression(s) because of the hypertrophic redevelopment of the original, especially in the paratexts, those deservedly notorious footnotes. But again, the sum total of the moves involved couldn't be more strategic and single-minded: the old core split and relocated, made to take marked positions. Marked and cleared, that is, for the reforegrounding of banality (the local love story actively excluding the subject) as Banality (the same love story but without the story: the story of the world, two of everything, played out enigmatically as Origin, in a symbolic Garden of Origins, at the heart of contemporary Milan). Life's rule thus gets deceivingly packaged as partly related and partly unrelated narratives delivering a structural maximum (a cohesive vision of human matter) through a structural minimum (a restriction of the only action set aside for noting as novelistic to the original scene: the revelation, the *tableau vivant* of the finale). It is a different Standard Oil the rival works for this time. Yet standards are standards, as the revamped old tale doesn't refrain from parading in those key closural (original) moves in the Garden. The standard bearer, in fact, bears them afresh each time, while the subject brings it all to bear in his work. Rather gluey, as always. But also totally line-pulling. Living matter authorially pulled to the exhaustion of all paragraphs and the exposure of the (welcome) End.

Resources

Alberto Godioli

Food resources (the cookery of the critic)

Literature, it is claimed, is the food of the mind. Sure enough, it brings delicious victuals, 'civo esquisitissimo' – although Gadda, self-ironically, jokes about it:

> And the critics will obtain some delicious food – I shall not say meal, which is more appropriate for hens. But like hens, once they come scratching about the copious dough of my papers, after pecking here and there, they will feel like beating their wings and fly. And indeed they will rise and become eagles in the sky. Or rather, they will become moral philosophers. (*Il primo libro delle Favole*, 1952 – PLF SGF II 78)

Irony aside, something about the association reading/eating (and writing/feeding) has always fascinated Gadda, partly as a compensatory fantasy for the hunger suffered in both World Wars, as well as during childhood – see *La cognizione del dolore* for the latter allegations. Back in 1932, in the preface to *Un fulmine sul 220*, an early novel destined to be published posthumously, he already portrayed literary critics as truffle-pigs: 'they don't read, they just "follow their nose" – like the pig when it should find truffles, and instead, under the oak, it only finds an acorn' (F220 13). Six years later, in announcing the forthcoming *Cognizione*, he would even envision the Shakespearean cauldron:

> 'Double, double toil and trouble: | Fire burn: and cauldron bubble' | A sort of magic tension comes to the boil in Gadda's cauldron, where creatures and shapes from the real world unexpectedly reappear to the surface. So, considering the way the author pitchforks his meat from time to time, one might think of lengthy cooking, of a pointless spell. (*Letteratura*, no. 5, 1938 – SGF I 1238)

After all, Gadda belongs to a long line of food suppliers exhibiting their provisions – Dante's *Banquet*, Rabelais' *Gargantua*, Giordano Bruno's *Ash Wednesday Supper* and Fielding's *Tom Jones* are cases in point:

> As we do not disdain to borrow wit or wisdom from any man who is capable of lending us either, we have condescended to take a hint from these honest victuallers, and shall prefix not only a general bill of fare to our whole entertainment, but shall likewise give the reader particular bills to every course which is to be served up in this and the ensuing volumes. The provision, then, which we have here made is no other than *Human Nature*. In reality, true nature is as difficult to be met with in authors, as the Bayonne ham, or Bologna sausage, is to be found in the shops. But the whole, to continue the same metaphor, consists in the cookery of the author.

For his part, Gadda may not be entirely honest: the client quite often gets something different – surprisingly different – from what is displayed in the shop window. However, he is also a resourceful victualler: the viands are hearty, varied and refined (Fielding would say) with 'the very quintessence of sauce and spices'. No wonder, then, that an increasing number of regular customers keep relying on the service especially since most of the menu got packaged as the chef's complete works in five courses plus indices – the Dante Isella edition 1988–93.

A special category of regulars is represented by the professional tasters (truffle pigs, if you prefer). Over the decades, the variety of Gadda's cuisine has enticed the most different sorts of gourmets from the most different palates – philology, narratology, linguistics, philosophy and comparative studies. But here our metaphor starts to break down, to some extent: are we just talking about *consumers*? Aren't critics too, in fact, *suppliers*? Good criticism is indeed a form of good cookery (it is, after all, a form of good writing). Its task is to enhance the main course, the primary literature, bringing out its taste without altering the original properties: useful side dishes for those wanting to explore, tactically, a main menu high in carbs. A side dish, yes – this is what we too, in producing this minimal guide, hope to provide. Not by chance, Gadda scholars have always claimed their rights in the field of the culinary arts by echoing their master's bent towards food-related metaphors. The first major essay published on our author was Gianfranco Contini's 'Carlo Emilio Gadda, o del *pastiche*' (1934, now Contini 1989: 3–10), and the word *pastiche* – French for *pasticcio*, a sort of pie made with many ingredients – soon became a widespread label. Gadda himself later took up the challenge, inventing his own exclusive mix, his *Pasticciaccio* (*de via Merulana*). Similarly, the term *macaronea*, originally referring to an eccentric form of Renaissance poetry, is often applied with reference to Gadda's linguistic experimentalism – for an excellent starter, see Albert Sbragia, *Carlo Emilio Gadda and the Modern Macaronic* (1996a). 'The macaroni have been served in my honour, and are waiting on the plate', Gadda stated in the essay 'Fatto personale o quasi' (1947 – VM SGF I 495), with a touch of sarcastic distrust and even alarm towards secondary cuisine, in case too many cooks might spoil his broth. He should have appreciated, however, that when the sous-chefs know their place things can only get tastier.

Given the wealth of secondary resources stacked in the Gadda larder, the risk of indigestion is undoubtedly there – how does one choose? Where can one start? There is no lack of starters even among the English dips and sauces. So, to cut on the number of times you send back the waiter before placing your order, here is our first round of recommendations. Sbragia (1996a) (just cited) – certainly rich. All main works come up to the surface and reveal their ingredients: linguistic expressionism, post-romantic *Angst*, modernist deformation, philosophical complexity and ambiguous satire – plenty of that. Then Bertone and Dombroski (1997): the classic appetiser selection. Gadda as humourist. Gadda and the baroque. Gadda's Freud. Gadda in the 1960s. Gadda and the form of the novel. The enigma of his grief. His murderous desires. And his mark of Cain too, for good measure. No one can go wrong with those *Contemporary Perspectives*, especially as they have somewhat matured through the work since carried out by the scholars involved in the project. And here is definitely one that we prepared earlier: out of the *Perspectives* came, in fact, Dombroski (1999) – *Gadda and the Baroque. Creative Entanglements*. This is the most demanding hors d'oeuvre, a real milestone in recent Gaddology. Our present vocabulary, our current theoretical approaches, the difficult art of our latest cuisine as critics – this slim book throws it all in.

In the exchanges over placing orders, this is also the moment when one should not overlook the specials – English menu still. For the lovers of fusion cuisine: Bouchard (2000), Di Martino (2007) and Wehling-Giorgi (2011) (focusing on Joyce, Céline and Beckett, and situating Gadda in the gastronomies of twentieth-century European fiction). For those instead who don't mind wondering whether digressions in novels are the plot: Santovetti (2007) and Pedriali (2011b) (reaching opposite conclusions from the same hilarious Sternian sound bite: 'Digressions, incontestably, are the sunshine'). Or what about admitting the worst case scenario, because all that happens at table is, in fact, but mild anthropophagy: Pedriali (2007b) (and if Italian is not too much for the stomach, also 2007a, or Spila 2011) – the idea here being that the immaterial world of the mind gets to know its share of pain in the cruel temptations of the kitchen.

The list could go on, but menus are menus and decisions must be taken. An interest, perhaps even less, a curiosity regarding the topic is bound, nowadays, to take us to Google and from Google to Edinburgh and the *Edinburgh Journal of Gadda Studies*. For the chance consumer turning savvy, the *EJGS* bill of fare will suit several kinds of tongues (Italian, English, German and French). Since 2000, the *Journal* proper has published eight regular issues and eleven special issues. The Archive comprises some two hundred critical essays, arranged thematically, including most of the classic early studies and the early reviews from the 1930s and 1940s. The selected primary Gadda offers one hundred large units of texts, while the secondary Bibliography, with over 1,800 entries, is the ultimate reference tool. There is, then, the *Pocket Gadda Encyclopedia*. If a website is hardly ever pocketable, the *Gadda Encyclopedia* will put you out of all pockets, what with growth (100 lemmas were published between 2002 and 2008, and now a print edition in 250 lemmas and four volumes is scheduled for 2013), what with networked content (the encyclopedia is the primary generator of those 30,000 links, present count, that make the *EJGS* one of most interconnected resources in the digital Humanities). Lastly, to round off this whistle-stop tour of the most exhaustive available *Art of Cooking Gadda. Made Plain and Easy* (title not referenced in our Bibliography, it is not even a virtual title): the latest *EJGS* release. This consists of the *EJGS* Decennial Special, almost a chunky soup of the day to face the coming (it is always coming) Scottish winter, and in it, soup within the soup, the *EJGS* Decennial Supplement. Some twenty essays by the leading experts in the field populate the four parts of this latest special issue, *EJGS* Supplement no. 9, like handfuls of healthy-option croutons, each section a label and a nutritious spoonful reflecting the inexhaustible elusiveness of our subject: *Impossible closure* (on Gadda's knack for unsolved contradictions), *Impure realism* (on his unorthodox way of representing reality), *Across genres* (on the contamination between codes and literary forms), *Uncommon readers* (on the author's heterogeneous reception and other reader-related issues). Navigating all of this is probably more than enough for a start, but we are insistent hosts – further guidance, we suspect, could still come in handy.

The (re)sources of complexity

Which is Gadda's best cooking trick? If there can be only one, then it must be complexity. Almost everything about Gadda is complex. Language, narrative structures, philosophical implications, even his most intimate and emotional stance. Yet at the very moment we cast complexity as the unerring law of this fiction, unexpected epiphanies of simplicity contradict our theories, thus altering (and paradoxically complicating) our picture. Ultimately, as Edgar Morin states in his *Introduction à la pensée complexe* (1990), 'complexity is a combination of simplicity and complexity' (our translation). In Gadda's case, there are definitely more (or less, for what it counts) things in his heaven and earth than are dreamt of in our philosophy. Flexibility, handling without rigidity (rather than just *with care*) would/should/could be the golden epistemic rule here. 'If we notice', this is how Morin sums it up, 'that the simplifying modes of knowledge mutilate reality more than they express it, if such modes of knowledge produce blindness rather than explanation, then a problem arises: how can we consider complexity in a non-simplifying way?' (Morin 1990: 9). For his part, being himself a resourceful dodger of lazy-fuzzy definitions, Gadda challenges us to be resourceful above all. In this sense, by staying loyal to the risks posed by the complex experience that goes under his name, some secondary resources might prove particularly useful – and this is why, here, we are again ready to assist.

If every text is, etymologically, a basketwork (Latin *textus*, from *texere* 'to weave'), compared to the average weaver Gadda looks like a non-Euclidean complication (*cum + plectere*, 'to weave, braid, twine'). His texts are, more precisely, *entanglements*. For Dombroski, the philosophical premises for such rich and useful metaphorical clusters must come from Gilles Deleuze's essay on Leibniz, *Le pli* (1988). Matter is indeed what folds, unfolds, refolds. We know the world (we know matter) because we enter the folds of events (time) by exploring the surface of folds (space). In Dombroski's argument, Gadda's texts are the modern equivalent of the Leibnizian baroque in as much as they try to seize reality in its folded complexity (etymology is still helping here: *plectere > pleat, piega, pli*) – nothing is plain and superficial in Gadda, despite everything getting spent on a surface, the surface of things. Words are never a transparent medium; their meanings are multiplied and distorted by historical and semantic stratifications. Events, in turn, stem from a multitude of converging causes, as Inspector Ingravallo explains at the beginning of *Pasticciaccio*: 'he also used words like knot, or tangle, or muddle, or *gnommero*, which in Roman dialect means skein' (QP RR II 16; *That Awful Mess*, 1985: 5).

Available in both English and Italian – indeed a double milestone – Dombroski (1999) is also entirely typical of the discipline. Gadda is complex matter, everything in his work gets tangled (interrelated): our lines of enquiry (language, style, contents, philosophy) must attempt to account for as much as it is critically (humanly) feasible of this totalising (omnivorous) take on reality. The groundbreaking effort, in this interpretive formula, was Roscioni (1969), whose paradigm of comprehensive methodology has been variously revisited, and sometimes productively contradicted in recent research (Bertoni 2001; Bonifacino 2002; Pedriali 2007a; Frasca 2011), without being superseded.

This approach spares us none of the specifics, of course: none of the specialised demands arising from specific areas of our author's work. In tackling the idea of complexity emerging from Gadda's philosophical manifesto *Meditazione milanese*, de Jorio Frisari (1996), Benedetti (2004a), Antonello (2005), Frasca (2011) and Porro (2011), for instance, underline the striking analogies between Gadda's thought and twentieth-century epistemological debates (from Gödel and Von Bertalanffy to Bateson and Morin). Specialist focus is all the more necessary in linguistic and stylistic analyses, given Gadda's proverbial arduousness particularly in this area – and here Emilio Manzotti, practically his entire output on Gadda, much of it now also available online in the *EJGS* Manzotti Archive, represents the point of reference. Even the biographical profile, as we shall see shortly, is the non-straightforward matter that either gets re-inflected by the wealth of new findings (the case relaunched by the Liberati Archives, at present, right at the heart of the Gadda Estate), or imposes the superior tactics of the overarching critical mystery (such as Roscioni's half biography of Gadda: why indeed stop at the year 1928?). However, complexity gets even more entrapped, crucial and central, and requires even greater critical commitment to a vast array of specifics, when it comes to the actual driving force of Gadda's writing – narration.

Until fairly recently, critics were viewing this entangled prose as evidence of an anti-narrative stance, a clear symptom of Gadda's lack of interest for telling stories, of his inability to deliver. Hence the stereotype, the *anti*-novelist, the nearly *unreadable* writer: a prejudice which is practically discredited now, thanks mostly to a better, fuller comprehension of complexity itself. Gadda's time, in many respects, has just come – high time it did. Understanding Gadda means now, and above all, reading him narratively; it means observing how painstakingly he interlaces themes and events, while building, in typical modernist fashion, on a realist tradition which he is bound to deform (Guglielmi 1997; Donnarumma 2006; Savettieri 2008; Baldi 2010; Godioli 2011). It implies a recognition of his peculiar joy (*joie*) of telling stories (Benedetti 2004b). It means, besides, to notice how these seemingly irregular plots conceal regular obsessive patterns, therefore creating a vital tension between complexity and diegetic functionality (Pedriali 2007a, 2007b). It is now clear that complexity doesn't necessarily bring to narrative chaos, or to a loss of textual consistency. It generates, rather, hypertexts – exactly like the web – and also hyper-novels (Riva 2002). This is why Gadda is ideally suited to the new web media; in this author, it is what gets connected through networks of internal links that becomes a unit of narrative, and a highly readable one at that.

What about biographical complexity itself? What about the *complexes*, the ambiguities, the tactics displayed over a lifetime? The tight connection between life and fiction gets seriously muddled, in this case, through a variety of filters – irony, obscurity, inconsistencies, contradictory behaviours:

> Mr Gadda (C. E.) is a long-time acquaintance of mine. Therefore my translation can be considered reliable and exact, at least as far as his ambiguous ways and manners allow. (From the pseudo-editorial commentary to *Il castello di Udine*, 1934 – CdU RR I 115)

Perhaps none of this should come as a surprise. Such ambiguities are only a particular form of complexity, and 'occur when two or more meanings of a statement do not agree among themselves, but combine to make clear a more complicated state of mind in the author' (Empson 1966: 133). Gadda's state of mind gets extremely complicated in nearly all respects, but some things do wind him up a lot more than others. Take a glaring example: his position regarding fascism. Our readers, being readers and viewers of *L'ingegner Gadda va alla guerra*, might find news of his support of the regime hard to believe. Yet Gadda was indeed a supporter, right from the early days, as his letters from Argentina, in that fateful 1922, reveal. In time, he did develop a form of revulsion for several aspects of fascism – his literature reveals this. *Il castello di Udine* and *La cognizione del dolore*, it cannot be denied, are texts from the 1930s, and express something a lot harsher than mere dissatisfaction. However, until the end of the Second World War, Gadda never officially questioned anything, and this was a surviving form of support, in the name of duty and diligence, as his technical writings promoting the technical side of fascism clearly show.

It was only in 1944–5, at the earliest count, namely at the time of writing *Eros e Priapo*, that Gadda's repressed intolerance burst open. Significantly, over time he did attempt to retro-date matters (SGF II 993–4), as far back as the early 1930s and earlier still. As Gifuni's rendition brilliantly suggests, the satirical fierceness of this text hides a truly Hamletic tangle of contradictory feelings: first and foremost a masochistic rage against that very part of himself that failed to recognise and oppose evil. Inevitably, critics have had to delve into this ideological mess. Why didn't Gadda criticise the regime before its fall? Or even why should we expect that he should? The situation, for a change, gets highly intricate, and forces us to revisit the basic antinomy fascism versus antifascism (Hainsworth 1997; Donnarumma 2002; Pedriali 2003; Stracuzzi 2007a; Savettieri 2009).

Family ties – the original regime – represent the other over-productive field of Hamletic ambivalence and dilemmatic polarisation. Examining how Gadda turns life (sources) into literature (resources) is the aim of the more searching enquiries into the author's early life (Roscioni 1997; Terzoli 2009). The younger brother Enrico, for instance, is regarded with a mix of unconditional love, admiration for his livelier personality and envy for his role as favourite son. After his death in the First World War, the survivor's feelings get even more contradictory, divided as they are between despair, jealousy and an irrational sense of guilt (Pedriali 2007b). The relation with the maternal figure can also be described in terms of duplicity and double bind; the lack of maternal love is perceived now as unjust deprivation, now as deserved punishment. Hence the constant fluctuations, from devotion to rage, from guilt to melancholy and abjection. Isolated and inept, rejected by women, unloved by Mother: quite unlike the other, the lively, the *apt*, the now dead *other*. No wonder this mental state, this acute case of a subjectivity convinced of having been cast for failure by destiny and by matter, the ultimate regime, informs the plots (the tangles), giving them their schema, their neat and even classical 'outcast complex' (Pedriali 2007a and 2007b). An entangled biography is thus the key to an entangled fiction. Paradoxically (but can we really be surprised?), a psychological *complex* does get *simplified* in the creative process that makes it narratable – which sends us straight back to complexity, Morin would agree, in an endless loop.

Genetic resources

But here is yet another take, before we hand over to Part II and the primary texts:

The Dinosaur escaped from the Museum and met the Lizard, who wasn't living there yet. 'Your day will come too', he said. (PLF SGF II 17)

Despite his long-time acquaintance with academies and museums, the Gaddasaurus is in great shape and evolving. His genetic complexity proves to be the real asset, the strongest evolutionary impulse coming from creative transmutations. Since Luca Ronconi's *Pasticciaccio* (1996) especially, Gadda has become an active resource for contemporary theatre and television. He even appears as a character in contemporary fiction and quasi-fiction (Enrique Butti's *Pasticciaccio argentino*, Alberto Arbasino's *L'Ingegnere in blu*, Tiziano Scarpa's *Comuni mortali*). The so-called *Gadda function* is fully plugged in, both in Italy and beyond Italy – for detailed bulletins, see Cortellessa (1998b), Donnarumma (2004) and Bouchard (2011).

Ultimately, it is those tangled texts that keep the Saurus healthy. Italo Svevo once argued that only if we consider ourselves (metaphorically) as *abbozzi* – sketches, drafts – shall we be able to keep open and available to our evolution. In Gadda studies, the ongoing, the unstoppable philological activity suggests that, like the original resurfacing magma, our extended work in progress suits this author to a T. It is not enough, not in his case, to have emerged once (Roscioni 1995b) and to have taken more or less shape (some thirty volumes of primary literature, to be precise). For instance, recent archival research has made a brand new edition of *Eros e Priapo* necessary (Pinotti 2007) as part of Adelphi's planned re-publication of Gadda's entire *opera omnia* – this barely twenty years on since Isella's complete edition of the *Opere*.

Gadda continues to be a story of looped opportunities, as Adelphi takes over Garzanti as Gadda's main publisher and the journal *I quaderni dell'ingegnere* returns to its regular publication cycle, which had been interrupted in 2007 following Dante Isella's death. The mainly philological approach of the *Quaderni* plays the ideal complement to the exegetical bent of the *EJGS*, and vice versa, in a framework of interchange between the two key methodological poles of the Gaddian critical act; any alteration of the textual reality modifies in fact our critical angle, while even the most allegedly neutral philological operation obviously implies interpretation.

The ontological and philological fluidity of Gadda's hypertexts favours, of course, their integration in the World Wide Web. To this effect, the *EJGS* has recently been joined by the Siena-based offline *Wiki Gadda* designed by Paola Italia. The platform was launched in 2011, with the primary aim of providing one common workspace for those labouring on the new edition of *Eros e Priapo* (2013) and the digitisation of the Liberati Archives. Once again, Gadda proves to be a driving force in the gradual migration of Italian – and not only Italian – literary studies to the web media. These are only glimpses of what the third millennium has in store for the Gadda enthusiasts, but this is also, probably and finally, enough to picture the sort of symbiotic bind that will keep the Saurus connected to his guards. In return for the nutritious resources he dispenses, we will continue to make ourselves useful by scratching his back, protecting him from the dust of the museums. With a bit of luck, the results will be as lasting and as evolving as those obtained by Adalgisa by scraping the deposits of Time off the back of a kitsch marble Chronos in the Monumentale Cemetery in Milan, at the close of the splendid hyper-novel that bears her name.

Endnote

Counting the dumplings. A short census

Gadda studies are a gluey interconnection of heterogeneous inputs and approaches, not unlike the real dumplings celebrated in *Meditazione milanese*:

> Dumplings are always oily, gluey, tied with cheese and sauces – one leads to a hundred more, each of them leads to a thousand more, each one of which leads to a million; and so on, *ad infinitum*. So much for cherries, each one of which – according to the experts – leads to another! (MM SVP 655)

Although a tough task to carry out even partially, some form of subject classification will be useful here, to identify the major trends and to give our readers the sense of where approximately to plunge the fork.

1. Original traumas: life and fiction

The biographical surveys tend to have a literary quality, possibly because Gadda's life, being a privileged key to his works, can also be seen as being organised by his fictions. This is the case of the first biographical landmark, Giulio Cattaneo's *Il gran Lombardo* (1973), mostly a rich collection of anecdotes on the later Gadda and explicitly inspired by Boswell's *Life of Samuel Johnson*. The same applies to *L'Ingegnere in blu* (2008) by Alberto Arbasino, himself a novelist and one that Gadda directly inspired. Roscioni (1997), *Il duca di Sant'Aquila*, the most significant biographical achievement thus far, takes us from childhood up to the late 1920s, engagingly combining factual reconstruction with sharp literary interpretation. Not dissimilarly, Terzoli (2009) examines the family photo album behind *Cognizione* arguing, among other things, that Gadda writes from photographs as well as from memory. Life and literature come quite specifically together again in the studies concerning Gadda's copious correspondence (Zancanella 1995; Scapinelli 2002; Carmina 2007), specific periods in Gadda's biography (such as the eighteen months spent in Argentina in the early 1920s – Grignani 1998; Bonifacino 2007; Bouchard 2011) and more importantly his experience in the First World War (Cortellessa 1998a; Terzoli 2001; Anglani 2004; Carmina 2008; Bertone 2009; Daniele 2009; Carta 2010; Bonifacino 2011; Cenati 2011).

Obsessive motifs, including the way these rely on literature and literary devices to express experience, get tackled in particular by Mileschi (2007) (war as a recurring metaphor), Pecoraro (1998) (the pervasive Manzonian justice), Pedriali (2007a, 2007b) (the outcast complex as an elaboration on Vergil's Palinurus). A proper use of psychoanalitic tools can prove particularly useful with a highly symptomatic writer like Gadda. Excellent examples in this area are Gioanola (2004) and Leucadi (2000) (both based on case histories with cross-checks to the texts), as well as Amigoni (1995) (a Freudian reading of *Pasticciaccio*) and Wieser (1995). Although Freud is undoubtedly the main reference point, alternative approaches are not lacking, such as Agosti's Lacanian interpretation of *Pasticciaccio* (1995) or Bertoni's remarks on the archetypical function of shadow in *Cognizione* (2011).

2. Political ambiguities: Gadda and fascism

The topic has remained notoriously controversial especially since Dombroski's (1984) essay (now Dombroski 1999: 117–34; see also Hainsworth 1997). In 2003 the *EJGS* deliberately issued two antithetical essays, 'Gadda fascista' and 'Gadda antifascista' (Hainsworth 2003 and Stellardi 2003) as part of Supplement *n* + 1, *Antinomie*, to complement its Supplement 2, *Eros o Logos? Il lungo sabato di Gadda*. The Saturday in question was the fascist one, and the primary material some ten articles published by Gadda in various degrees of explicit praise of the technologies of the regime. These articles had not made it to the Garzanti edition of the *Opere*; the material is now available in print edition as well (Bertone 2005; see also Stracuzzi 2007a). A censored version of the first chapters from *Eros e Priapo* has also since been published (Italia and Pinotti 2008). Other relevant work includes a reconsideration of Gadda's early attitude towards fascism, building on new textual evidence from the Garzanti Archives (Savettieri 2009). Interestingly, in the system of looped opportunities that is the trademark of this story, *Eros e Priapo* was among the first texts to come out of Garzanti ownership, giving Paola Italia and Giorgio Pinotti the all clear for the publication of the *Eros e Priapo* no one has yet read, this at a time which was and continues to be politically ripe for Fabrizio Gifuni's take on the text.

3. 'In the beginning was . . .': language and philosophy

Two critics and two publications have shaped Gadda studies. By 1934 Gianfranco Contini had a classification to offer, and did offer it in the form of a long review of *Il castello di Udine*, Gadda's second book. In his authoritative view (Contini would soon become one of Italy's leading literary critics), Gadda's deformation and plurilingualism were a clear case of *pastiche*, or *maccheronea*. The first two keywords in our vocabulary had thus been activated, initiating a lasting enquiry into Gadda's language. Then Gian Carlo Roscioni broke new grounds in 1969 with his seminal *La disarmonia prestabilita*. This was the first systematic analysis of the philosophical implications of Gadda's writings; his original dialogue with Leibniz finally came to the fore, together with his passion for a plurality of causes, for reality as an intricate *knot*. Five years later, in 1974, one year after Gadda's death, Roscioni would underpin his work with the edition of *Meditazione milanese*, the philosophical treatise Gadda had penned in 1928 and never published.

Language and philosophy have battled it out ever since, at the same time becoming less polarised fields of enquiry into our subject. Both methods have remained useful and productive in their separate ways, as proved by many remarkable examples. Cesare Segre, for instance, has reconsidered the expressive variety of Gadda's language through the Bakhtinian concepts of polyphony and the carnevalesque (Segre 1985 and 2001). Dante Isella, for his part, has linked the Gadda linguistic phenomenon to the great tradition of Lombard expressionism (Isella 1994). McConnell (1973) and Italia (1998) have respectively analysed the rich lexical texture of the Roman and Milanese Gadda. Other works focus on single stylistic devices, such as neologisms (Matt 2004, with regard to *Eros e Priapo*), scientific vocabulary (Zublena 2002), irony and parody (Turolo 1995; Italia 1996) or syntax (Manzotti 1997; Ponticelli 2004). With the passing of time, linguistic issues have been increasingly connected to other features of Gadda's writing: the *pastiche*, for instance, is now considered the direct outcome of the author's entangled theories on cognition and narration (Sbragia 1996a, 1996b; Donnarumma 2001; Segre 2001; Stracuzzi 2002).

Also among the studies concerning Gadda's thought the perspectives have moved on and are now much more varied and integrated. Some focus on Gadda's properly philosophical works, such as *Meditazione milanese* (de Jorio Frisari 1996; Casini 2004) or the unfinished dissertation on Leibniz (Minazzi 2006; Stracuzzi 2007b). Others have tried to detect the links with some of the major scientists and thinkers from the last two centuries, from Darwin to Freud in particular (Lucchini 1994 and 1997; Antonello 2004; Frasca 2011; Porro 2011). Another line of enquiry compares Gadda's innovative stance to current trends in epistemology and cognitive sciences (Benedetti 2004a; Porro 2009; Bernini 2011). Aside from the strictly philosophical analyses, Roscioni's legacy has also had an effect on broader attempts to define Gadda's poetics, meant as a coherent way of conceiving and representing reality. An especially representative case is the much cited Dombroski (1999), where the key notion of the baroque, revisited through Deleuze, is used to explain central Gadda tenets (knowledge as deformation, subject decentrement, linguistic contamination). Bertoni (2001) (on Gadda's own invention of reality) and Bonifacino (2002) (on the epistemic and moral antinomy between truth and appearance) are other good samples of the attempt to isolate, partly following Roscioni, a solid core under the fluid and fleeting substance of the texts. A peculiar position, in this respect, is held by Stellardi (2006), who expressly rejects – precisely on account of such fluidity – the idea of using the term *poetics* with reference to this author.

4. *Reading for the plot: Gadda, Modernism and narration*

Going back to dates. 1970: *La meccanica* (M RR II 461–589), the novel drafted in 1928, finally sees the light of day. A year later it is the turn of another narrative sketch from the 1920s, *Novella seconda* (NS RR II 1027–69). 1983: Dante Isella publishes *Racconto italiano di ignoto del novecento* (RI SVP 381–613), Gadda's first proper literary attempt, not by chance a novel, as well as an intense reflection on the novelist's tools. The years in question: 1924–5. 1987: Emilio Manzotti publishes the annotated edition of *La cognizione* (Gadda 1987), complete with unpublished material. Other milestones in recent publication history – Garzanti's *Opere* (1988–93) and the unfinished *Un fulmine sul 220* (2000) – confirm Gadda's uninterrupted commitment to narration, both large and small scale. It is no surprise, then, that during the last two decades Gadda has been increasingly interpreted as a modernist storyteller. This doesn't imply a devaluation of the components identified previously, language and philosophy – the framework is simply getting wider. Some remarkable critical achievements in this respect date back to the 1990s; Sbragia (1996a) and Guglielmi (1997), in particular, variously focus on Gadda's peculiar dialogue with the realist tradition, comparing him to other milestones of European modernist fiction (Joyce, Céline, Pirandello, Svevo). These topics would soon be developed by other important studies such as Donnarumma (2001 and 2006), Dombroski (2003), Lugnani (2004), Savettieri (2008), Baldi (2010), each providing useful cues to Gadda's attitude to narration with regard to the modernist distortion of nineteenth-century realism. For those who want to go beyond the modernist-centred approach, Carla Benedetti underlines the author's original way of considering human events from the perspective of natural history, thus redefining the very concept of plot (Benedetti 1995 and 2011), while Federica Pedriali's intratextual surveys unveil the strong diegetic function played by recurring themes and structures, what she calls Gadda's narremes and plot builders (Pedriali 2007a and 2007b). On the narrative strategies employed in given texts, instead, it will be useful to focus especially on *Pasticciaccio* (Stracuzzi 2001; Pedriali 2004 and 2011b; Santovetti 2007) and on the handling of the short-story form (Sarina 2001; Kleinhans 2005; Cenati 2010; De Michelis 2010). Lastly, a large number of intertextual analyses points out the complex links with crucial narrative models like Manzoni (Pecoraro 1996; Bologna 1998; Ponticelli 2003), Balzac (Rinaldi 2001), Dickens (Godioli 2011), Dostoevsky (Adamo 2004), d'Annunzio (Zollino 1998; Papponetti 2002).

5. Gadda revisited: from early reception to lasting influence

The critical verdicts from the 1930s and 1940s were bound to shape the early Italian reception; the first detailed account in this regard comes from Stracuzzi (2007c), while Ungarelli (1993b) and Andreini (2004) focus on the circulation among the general reading public. Regarding the early circulation abroad and the broader issue of translatability (including authorial translation from concept to text), the recommended critical line-up should include: Weaver (1989), Clerico (1993), Riatsch (1995), Stellardi (1995), de Lucca (1999 and 2002), Cortellessa (2001), Camps (2002) and Pinotti (2009).

Gadda's influence on younger writers has been very considerable, the author notwithstanding ('Mr Gadda is by no means responsible for what his self-proclaimed "followers" do' – 1960 interview, Gadda 1993: 72). Several generations, from the so-called *engineer's nephews* (Arbasino, Pasolini and Testori), back in the 1960s, up to present-day literature, have variously interpreted this primary material. The questions for us are to what extent this adds to the study of our author and whether we think that creative misunderstandings prove Gadda to be a working model – the phrase *funzione Gadda* may be ubiquitous now but requires that we tackle exactly such issues (Cortellessa 1998b; Donnarumma 2004). This is all the more pressing because of the success of a special category of creative readings: the *intersemiotic* translation to other media. Even more than his interpreters, it is indeed Gadda's texts, not meant as they were for either the cinema or the theatre, that prove how well and even how easily this experimentalism can travel. Germi's 1959 movie *Un maledetto imbroglio*, based on *Pasticciaccio*, has been studied from this perspective by Gutkowski (2002) and Fracassa (2011); Luca Ronconi's stunning 1996–7 production for stage and television has also been widely commented (Longhi 1996 and 2001a; Andreini and Tessari 2001; Cortellessa 2002; D'Antoni 2008). And, of course, having taken Italy by storm, Fabrizio Gifuni's *L'ingegner Gadda va alla guerra* is beginning to claim its share of critical attention (Genna 2012).

6. Establishing the text: philology and the state of the archives

'Is there a text in this class?', Stanley Fish asked provokingly back in 1996. Literary interpretation has the power to multiply texts, especially when handling a plural writer like Gadda. Yet, despite the temptation of plurality, any legitimate hermeneutic operation must start from a single, philologically reliable source. In Gadda's case, this was particularly urgent, due to the *messy* condition of both the outputs published in his lifetime and the many works in progress that have emerged since his death. Sorting out this tangle as far as it is possible is still the primary aim of much of the philological work carried out at present. The Garzanti edition of the (almost) complete works directed by Dante Isella brought together a number of top philologists and scholars (Paola Italia, Emilio Manzotti, Clelia Martignoni, Giorgio Pinotti, Claudio Vela et al.), establishing the landmark in this respect, and indeed setting the standards for editing much of the contemporary Italian canon.

But landmarks and milestones, when the material is rich, make disciplines even more expansive. At present, Gaddian philology is reaching new peaks of editorial activity as Adelphi schedules a philological overhaul of the entire opus while the Liberati Archives, thanks to

Arnaldo Liberati's commitment to the welfare of the subject on behalf of the Gadda Estate, continue to reveal masses of previously unseen and extremely precious *gaddiana*, ranging from personal effects in the author's possession at the time of death to typescripts and other works in progress that had been assumed lost (Italia 2004 and 2007; Pinotti 2007; Colli 2010). This buzz of activity, marked as it is by milestones, is bound to feed the particularly circular life of our subject, as in Escher's famous lithograph, where one hand (the philologist's? the interpreter's?) draws the other, so that the other may draw in turn.

PART II

L'ingegner Gadda va alla guerra
o della tragica istoria di Amleto Pirobutirro

Drammaturgia originale di Fabrizio Gifuni
(da Carlo Emilio Gadda e William Shakespeare)

Gadda goes to war
or The tragic story of Hamlet Pirobutirro

An original drama by Fabrizio Gifuni
(Based on Carlo Emilio Gadda and William Shakespeare)

Translated into English by Christopher John Ferguson and Cristina Olivari
Revised by Lucinda Byatt, Federica G. Pedriali and Silvana Vitale

1. Incipit

L'attore entra dal fondo della scena. Sistema la sua sedia. Prende a tracciare delle linee immaginarie sul palcoscenico (un asse delle ascisse e uno delle ordinate, che costituiranno nel corso dello spettacolo il suo spazio 'amletico'). Dopo qualche attimo la sua voce prende a sdoppiarsi in due voci. La prima è quella di Polonio, e ha una strana 'erre' arrotata, l'altra è quella del Principe Amleto e ha un vago accento lombardo.

PqLONIO

Cosa leggiamo, mio signore?

AMLETO

Verba . . . verba . . .

PqLONIO

Vermi?

AMLETO

Ma no! Non ver-mi: Ver-ba! In latino vuol dire parole. Parole, parole, parole . . .

PqLONIO

Ah . . . e qual è la materia?

AMLETO

Carta . . . pecora . . .

PqLONIO

Intendevo, che argomento.

1. Incipit

The actor enters from the back of the stage. He places his chair. He traces imaginary lines on the stage (x and y axes that will make up his Shakespearean space during the play). After a moment his voice begins to split into two distinct voices. The first is that of Polonius, who has a strange, rolling 'r', the other is that of Prince Hamlet: his has a vaguely Lombard accent.

PoLONIUS
What are you reading, my lord?

HAMLET
Words, words . . .

PoLONIUS
Worms?

HAMLET
No, Words! Verba! Lexis! Parole! Words!

PoLONIUS
Ah . . . and what is the matter?

HAMLET
Paper . . . parchment . . .

PoLONIUS
I mean, the matter you read, my lord?

AMLETO

Infamie! Questo umorista randagio pretende che i vecchi abbiano barba grigia, occhi incispati di resina, non senza penuria di cervello e grande fiacchezza di lombi . . . cose tutte che credo e arcicredo; ma ascrivo a disonestà metterle giù a stampa; perché, tanto, anche voi diverrete vecchio come me, se vi riesce di andare all'indietro come un granchio.

POLONIO

Per pazzo che sia non manca di metodo . . .

Dopo una pausa, come continuando il suo immaginario dialogo, la 'voce del Principe' aggiunge:

Senza stagione la vita, e senza gioia: e la volontà di bene, la rinuncia, la pena profonda: vedute solo da Dio, dal fondo abissale di quel suo cazzioso caleidoscopio, dove le figurazioni si succedevano pazzamente le une alle altre, come sempre rinnovate e deformanti costellazioni di pidocchi, preda d'un rapido annullamento, aggiudicatarie di un eterno castigo. La volontà di bene non riconosciuta e non rimeritata dai contubernali, se non di sputi e di lazzi. 'Interventista stronzo, volontario di guerra, pera marcia, scrittore di sciocchezze, borghese! . . .'

HAMLET

Slanders, sir! For the satirical rogue says here that old men have grey beards, their eyes purging thick amber and plum-tree gum, and that they have a plentiful lack of wit, together with most weak hams. All of which, sir, though I most powerfully and potently believe, yet I hold it not honesty to have it thus set down; for you yourself, sir, should be old as I am, if like a crab you could go backward.

POLONIUS

Though this be madness, yet there is method in't.

After a pause, as if continuing his imaginary dialogue, the 'voice of the Prince of Denmark' adds:

Life is without season, without joy. The yearning for good, renouncing it, the dolorous suffering: all seen by God alone, from the abysmal bottom of his cantankerous kaleidoscope, where the configurations madly followed on another, like ever-novel and deforming constellations of lice, destined for a swift annihilation, for the eternal punishment bestowed upon them. The yearning for good that is never recognised, never rewarded by comrades, if not by sputum and teasing. 'Bastard of an Interventionist! You happily volunteered for service! Bad apple! Writer of nonsense! Bourgeois! . . .'

2. I diari

Sempre scisso in due voci, l'attore continua il suo immaginario dialogo . . .

POLONIO

. . . pera marcia? . . . pera butirro: . . . Pirobutirro!

AMLETO

. . . Dalla lavagna della mia memoria io cancellerò tutti i triviali, frivoli ricordi, tutti i detti dei libri, tutte le forme, tutte le impressioni passate, che la giovinezza e l'osservazione graffiarono quivi; e il tuo comandamento tutto solo vivrà nel libro e nel volume del mio cervello, senza vile materia che l'infetti; sì, per il cielo!

Parte un canto degli alpini . . . Da questo momento, il Nostro sprofonderà nel pozzo nero della sua memoria . . . (Ma ogni tanto, nel corso del racconto, le due voci – assieme a una terza, quella della MADRE *– riaffioreranno.)*

Il bollettino del Ministero della guerra del giorno 5 agosto 1915 mi nominava, dietro mia richiesta del 27 marzo ultimo scorso, sottotenente nella milizia territoriale, arma di fanteria, con destinazione al 5° Alpini. Il comando reggimentale di Milano a cui mi presentai il 17 agosto mi destinò al Magazzino di Edolo. Il 18 sera ero a Edolo, dopo aver prestato il giuramento a Milano. Presi alloggio all'albergo Derna, dove sono tutt'ora, e cominciai tosto il servizio, o più precisamente l'istruzione.

Edolo, 24 agosto 1915

Le note che prendo a redigere sono stese addirittura in buona copia, come vien viene, con quei mezzi lessigrafici, grammaticali e stilistici che mi avanzeranno dopo la sveglia antelucana, le istruzioni, le marce, i pasti copiosi, il vino e il caffè. Scrivo sul tavolino incomodo della mia

2. The diaries

Still split in two voices, the actor continues his imaginary dialogue . . .

POLONIUS
. . . Bad apple? . . . bad pear! pirum malum: . . . Pirobutirro!

HAMLET
. . . Yea, from the table of my memory I'll wipe away all trivial fond records, all saws of books, all forms, all pressures past, that youth and observation copied there, and thy commandment all alone shall live within the book and volume of my brain, unmix'd with baser matter. Yes, yes by heaven.

Cue a marching song of the Alpini . . . At this moment, our hero falls into the black well of his memory . . . (But every so often, in the course of the story, the two voices – along with a third, that of the MOTHER *– will resurface.)*

The Ministry of War bulletin of 5th August 1915, named me, following my request of 27th March last, as Second Lieutenant in the territorial militia, infantry, assigned to the 5th Alpine Regiment. The Regimental Command in Milan, to whom I presented myself on 17th August, sent me to the storerooms at Edolo. The evening of the 18th, I was at Edolo, after taking my oath in Milan. I took a room at the Hotel Derna, where I am still, and soon began my service, or more precisely my training.

Edolo, 24th August 1915
The notes that I set down here are in fair copy, but they are as they come, with those orthographical, stylistic and grammatical means that I have left to me after the pre-dawn reveille, drills, marches, copious meals, wine and coffee. I write at the uncomfortable table in my room,

stanza, all'albergo Derna, verso le una e mezza pomeridiana. Le imposte chiuse e i vetri aperti mi lasciano entrare l'aria fresca e quasi fredda della montagna, i rumori dei trasporti e le voci della gente: mi impediscono la veduta di un muro, che si trova a due o tre metri in faccia e in cui non figurano che finestre chiuse, e delle rocce del Baitone.

Sto abbastanza bene di corpo, per quanto il troppo cibo preso ieri alla mensa e l'uso che vi si fa di vino e caffè, a cui io non ho l'abitudine, mi lascino un senso di odiosa sazietà e di intorpidimento intellettuale: ho anche un po' di sonno. Quest'aria fresca mi ristora e un po' di raccoglimento mi fa piacere.

Spiritualmente sono seccato dalla mancanza di notizie della mia famiglia, poiché da quando sono a Edolo, cioè dal 18 corrente, non ho ricevuto una riga; dal continuo seccarmi che il capitano fa (e con ragione) perché mi provveda del cinturone di cuoio e del revolver; dalla perdita dei miei guanti, che occorrono all'istruzione e che difficilmente potrò sostituire. Penso raramente alla guerra, non per indifferenza, ma per timore di soffrir troppo nella preoccupazione e anche perché ne sono continuamente distratto dalla vita giornaliera.

Edolo, sabato 28 agosto 1915

Breve diario: stamane sveglia alle 5. Istruzione in piazza d'armi. Comandai il plotone in ordine chiuso, in ordine sparso, e nella scuola di compagnia. Fui lodato per voce chiara, forte, e per essere ormai discretamente esperto. Fisicamente continua il disturbo gastro-intestinale; nervosismo, irrequietezza, idee noiose; moralmente un po' di malessere, poi nullità e tranquillità. Spero nel riposo e nella quiete. In complesso però, salvo il disturbo intestinale, sto molto bene. I compagni talora un po' noiosucci: pettegolezzi, sofismi del pittore genovese Marchini, sottotenente antimilitarista, bestialità monotone di Brugnoli. In fondo buona gente.

Edolo, 31 agosto 1915

Ieri tosatura a zero dei capelli. Mi coricai presto la sera. Stamane grande sonnolenza. Cattive notizie dal fronte Russo mi avvilirono assai e mi resero triste. Anche l'insuccesso di una nostra azione sul Tonale mi rattristò; vi perirono una trentina di soldati e quattro ufficiali, due capitani e due sottotenenti: quale proporzione!

Edolo, 2 settembre 1915

Hodie quel vecchio Gaddus e duca di Sant'Aquila arrancò du' ore per via sulle spallacce del monte Faetto, uno scioccolone verde per castani, in the Hotel Derna, around one thirty in the afternoon. The closed shutters and open windows let the cool, almost cold mountain air, the noise of the traffic and the voices of people into the room: the shutters block my view of a wall that is facing me, two or three metres away, revealing nothing but closed windows and the rocks of the Corno Baitone.

I feel fairly well – in myself – even though I ate too much at the mess yesterday, and the quantities of wine and coffee – something I'm not used to – leave me with a hateful sense of satiety and intellectual torpor: I am also rather sleepy. This cool air refreshes me, and I enjoy the odd moment of reflection.

Spiritually, I am annoyed by the lack of news of my family, because since I came to Edolo, namely since the 18th of this month, I have not received so much as a line; the constant bother the Captain gives me (and rightly so) so that I kit myself out with a big leather belt and revolver; the loss of my gloves, which I need for training, and which will be difficult to replace. I rarely think of the war, not because of indifference, but for fear of suffering too much in worrying and also because I am constantly distracted by everyday life.

Edolo, Saturday, 28th August 1915
A short entry: reveille this morning at 5. Drill in the parade ground. I led the platoon in close order, in mixed order, and in the whole company on parade. I was praised for my clear, strong voice, and for being quite an expert by now. Physically, my gastro-intestinal troubles are still present; nervousness, restlessness, noisome ideas, a little moral malaise, then emptiness and serenity. I wish for rest and quiet. Overall, however, excepting my intestinal worries, I'm very well. My companions are a little dull. Gossips. Marchini, a Genovese painter and anti-militaristic Second Lieutenant, is full of sophistry; then there is the monotone brutishness of Brugnoli: basically good people.

Edolo, 31st August 1915
Yesterday: the shearing. I went to bed early. Very sleepy this morning. Bad news from the Russian front has disheartened and saddened me. Also the failure of our action on the Tonale saddened me; we lost about thirty soldiers and four officers, two captains and two lieutenants. What a proportion!

Edolo, 2nd September 1915
On this day, Old Gaddus, Duke of Sant'Aquila trudged for two hours up the shoulders of Mount Faetto, a great big green fool, through fields,

prati, e conifere, come dicono i botanici, e io lo dico perché di lontano non distinsi se larici o se abeti vedessi. Ahi che le rupi dure e belle del corno Baitone si celavano nelle nubi, forse per ira della non giusta preferenza data ai rosolacci. Ma è destino che chi vuole non possa, e chi può non voglia. Ora, questo Gaddus amerebbe adunghiare questo Baitone, ma gli è come carne di porco, a volerla mangiare di venerdì: Moisè ti strapazza. Ora, questo è il venerdì, perché è il tempo delle mortificazioni, e Baitone è porco, perché piace, e il generale Cavaciocchi, buon bestione, è Moisè, perché non vuole. E il Gaddus è il pio credente nella legge, e nella sua continova sanzione. Per che detto Duca seguitò per prati e boschive forre la sua buona mandra, che lungo la costa cantò nel silenzio della valle. Cantò la canzone dell'alpino che torna, poi che chi non torna né pure avanza fiato a cantare, e che gli è chiesto come s'è cambiato in viso dell'antico colore: è stato il sole del Tonale che mi ha cambià il colore *(accennando il canto)*, rispose l'alpino: e la sua ragazza si contenta.

Edolo, 7 settembre 1915

Notte agitata da sogni tristi: è forse il primo sogno di guerra che ho fatto. Da casa ho buone notizie. Con tutto ciò una grande tristezza mi domina, e nulla vale a scuoterla: l'isolamento spirituale, (poiché nessuno dei miei colleghi è persona con cui possa interamente affiatarmi), la non perfetta calma de' miei nervi, la non perfetta vicenda de' miei giorni, alternati di riposo annoiato e di fatica, di notizie discrete e di cattive, sono la causa principale del mio stato: poi la lontananza dalla famiglia comincia a farsi sentire. Oltre tutto, i miei compagni genovesi hanno preso a bersagliarmi con scherzi spesso indiscreti: l'altra sera mi piovvero in camera mentre già dormivo e mi misero tutto a soqquadro: nulla di male. Ma alla mensa continuano, continuano, con una insistenza asfissiante: io, che pure sono così facile all'allegria e allo scherzo, alle burle di ogni genere, ne sono arcistufo. Alla prima che mi dicono ancora mi alzo da tavola e me ne vado: perché sono troppo annoiato. Quale è la ragione psicologica di questa mia attuale intolleranza? Io la ricerco principalmente nella diversità di carattere: infatti se il carattere de' miei allegri persecutori fosse simile al mio, e se il loro scherzo si fermasse là dove deve ragionevolmente fermarsi non come qualità, ma almeno rispetto al tempo, io accetterei in buona pace tutto. Ma l'uno di costoro, certo Adolfo Trinchero, viaggiatore di commercio e sportmann, che pronuncia Wagner all'italiana, come Agnese, è un carattere duro, che ha dei momenti soltanto di scarsa affabilità o meglio di buon umore: duro coi

chestnuts and coniferophyta, as the botanists say, and I say this because from a distance I could not make out whether they were larches or silver firs. Alas! The hard and beautiful rocks of the Baitone concealed themselves in the clouds, perhaps angry at the preference shown unjustly to the poppies. But such is Fate: those who want to, can't; and those who can, don't want to. Now, this Gaddus would love to grab the Baitone, but it is to him like eating pork on a Friday: Moses tells you off. This is Friday, the time for mortification, and the Baitone is pork because I like it, and General Cavaciocchi, that good old beast, is Moses, because he doesn't want me to. And Gaddus is the pious believer in the law, and in its continual sanction. So, the said Duca followed, through fields and wooded ravines, his good herd, which, across the hillside, sang in the silence of the valley. They sang the song of the Alpino who comes back – since those who don't come back don't have the breath to sing – and is asked why the colour of his face has changed: it was the sun of the Tonale that changed my colour (*humming the tune*), says the Alpino: and his girl is happy at that.

Edolo, 7th September 1915

A restless night and sad dreams: perhaps the first war dream I have ever had. I have good news from home. With all this, a great sadness looms over me, and nothing can shake it off: spiritual isolation (because none of my colleagues are people I can entirely get along with), the not-perfect calm of my nerves, the not-perfect series of my days, alternating as they do between boring repose and hard work, between news and bad news; these are the principal causes of the state I am in: then the family are so far away. On top of all that my Genovese comrades have taken to targeting me with jokes that are often indiscreet: the other night they stormed into my room while I was asleep and left everything in disorder: no harm done. But in the mess, they keep on, keep on with a suffocating insistence: I, who myself am so easily given to high spirits and jokes, larks of any kind, am royally sick of it . . . The first thing they say to me, I'll get up from the table and go: because it's too, too boring. What is the psychological reason for my current intolerance? I locate it primarily in the difference between our characters: indeed, if the character of my merry persecutors was similar to mine, and if the joke were to stop where it reasonably should, if not in terms of quality at least in terms of time, I would accept everything in good humour. But one of them, a certain Adolfo Trinchero, travelling salesman and sportsman, who pronounces Wagner as an Italian word, like lasagna, is a tough character, who has only moments of limited cordiality, or rather of good humour: hard on

soldati, coi colleghi: desideroso di cogliere la gente in fallo: tirchio nel suo meschino giudizio, tanto da giudicare strisciante la mia condotta perché saluto con deferenza i superiori, dei quali, fuori servizio, mi infischio altamente.

L'altro è l'anarchico Tolstoiano, spirito libero e fine, come vuol farsi credere: in realtà superficiale nel giudizio e pieno di idee secche. Exempla: solo la musica tedesca e russa è bella; il Manzoni è un rifrittore di roba vecchia e io sono un bamboccio ripetitore di lezioni scolastiche perché mi son permesso citarlo fra i grandi milanesi. Io credo che i miei compagni si son fatti della mia levatura intellettuale la seguente idea: minchione, perché non parlo e qualche volta faccio delle domande ingenue (per vedere come rimangono gli altri), e perché accetto troppo gli scherzi, per pigrizia e anche per non provocare bizze o malumori, il che reputo un dovere; buon geometra che non vede al di là dell'ettaro; teorema di Pitagora, macchina a vapore, un po' di campanelli elettrici, polo positivo e polo negativo. Si sentono dire poi certe castronerie, e si voltano a me per intontirmi; e io dico: 'ah?' quando mi parlano, in generale perché i particolari sono spinosi, di poeti, di questi o di questi altri. Il tolstoiano Marchini è pittore, di paesaggio, a sua detta esteta, ecc. ecc.; ma non sa schizzare una figura con un lapis. A dirgli: 'ho fatto una bella camminata', proposizione innocente, non è vero?, ti salta addosso come un mastino, a dirti che ne ha fatta una doppia, in minor tempo, che è skiatore, ecc. ecc. ecc. E io dico: 'sì, sì, sì, già, già' e torno al mio piatto melanconicamente.

Il ten. Pozzi, invece, l'altro giorno morì mentre, uscito dalle nostre posizioni per ridurre ai compagni la salma di un ucciso, pur sapendo di arrischiare la vita, era già presso il cadavere. Colpito dalla fucileria austriaca mentre era aggrappato alle rocce, rovinò nel vuoto. Il ten. Pechini, del 5° Genio, recuperò con pari pericolo la salma d'un caporale, tornando incolume. Pechini era l'altro ieri alla mensa con noi. Pagnanelli ci rallegra col suo spirito romanesco, con le sue porcheriole e storielle comicissime, in fondo alle quali con voce precipitosa e serissimo, domanda: 'Hai cabido il dobbio senso?'

Edolo, 20 settembre 1915

I nostri uomini sono calzati in modo da far pietà: scarpe di cuoio scadente e troppo fresco per d'uso, cucite con filo leggero da abiti anzi che con spago, a macchina anzi che a mano. Dopo due o tre giorni di uso si aprono, si spaccano, si scuciono, i fogli delle suole si distaccano

the soldiers, and with colleagues: ready to find fault with people: stingy and petty in his judgements, so much so that he judges my conduct to be servile because I salute my superiors with deference; people who, when I'm not in uniform, I don't give a damn for.

The other is a Tolstoyan anarchist, a free, elevated spirit, or so he would like us to believe: in reality, he is superficial in his judgement and full of dead ideas. *Exempli gratia*: only German and Russian music is beautiful; Manzoni is a rehasher of old stuff and I'm a little kid who repeats his school lessons just because I called him one of Milan's greatest citizens. I believe that my comrades have formed the following idea of my intellectual stature: I'm an arse, because I don't speak out and sometimes pose naive questions (to see how the others react), and because I put up with jokes too much, out of laziness and also so as to avoid scenes or causing resentment, which I consider a duty. The humble surveyor who does not see beyond the hectare; the Pythagorean theorem, the steam engine, a few electric bells, positive and negative poles. So some nonsense is said, and they turn to me, trying to piss me off, and I say 'huh?' when they talk to me – in general terms because the particulars are tricky – about poets, about this or that. The Tolstoyan, Marchini, is a painter. Of landscapes. He calls himself an aesthete, etc. etc., but cannot sketch a figure with a pencil. If you say to him, 'I had a nice walk' – an innocent proposition, is it not? – he jumps on you like a mastiff, to tell you he did double the walk in less time, that he's a skier, etc. etc. etc. And I say, 'yeah, yeah uh-huh, hmm' and I return melancholically to my meal.

Lieutenant Pozzi, meanwhile, died the other day having left our position to rescue the body of a slain comrade, knowing that he was risking his life. He was almost beside the body. Shot by Austrian rifle fire while clinging to the rocks, he fell into space. Lieutenant Pechini, of the 5th Sappers, ran similar risks to recover the body of a corporal, returning unharmed. Pechini was at the mess with us the other day. Pagnanelli cheers us up with his Roman sense of humour, his off-colour jokes, his funny stories, at the end of which he asks, with a hasty voice and looking dead serious: 'Geddit?'

Edolo, 20th September 1915
Our men are shod in such a pitiful way: leather that is too fresh and of too poor a quality to use, sewn with thread that is too fine, by machine rather than by hand. After two or three days of use the shoes burst open, they rip, they tear, and the sheets of the soles peel apart in the damp. A

nell'umidità l'uno dall'altro. Un mese di servizio le mette fuori d'uso. Questo fatto ridonda a totale danno, oltre che dell'economia dell'erario, del morale delle truppe costrette alla vergogna di questa lacerazione, e, in guerra, alle orribili sofferenze del gelo! Quanta abnegazione è in questi uomini così sacrificati a 38 anni, e così trattati! Come scuso, io, i loro brontolamenti, la loro poca disciplina! Essi portano il vero peso della guerra, peso morale, finanziario, corporale, e sono i peggio trattati. Quanto delinquono coloro che per frode o per incuria li calzano a questo modo; se ieri avessi avuto innanzi un fabbricatore di calzature, l'avrei provocato a una rissa, per finirlo a coltellate.

'Chi è là? Un topo . . .? Un topo! Morto per un ducato!' 'Ah . . . sono morto.'

Noi Italiani siamo troppo acquiescenti al male; davanti alle cause della nostra rovina diciamo: 'Eh ben!', e lasciamo andare. Non è esagerazione il riconoscere come necessaria una estrema sanzione per i frodatori dell'erario in questi giorni, poiché il loro delitto, oltre che frode, è rovina morale dell'esercito. Io mi auguro che possano morir tisici, o di fame, o che vedano i loro figli scannati a colpi di scure. Chissà quelle mucche gravide, quegli acquosi pancioni di ministri e di senatori e di generaloni: chissà come crederanno di aver provveduto alle sorti del paese con i loro discorsi, visite al fronte, interviste, ecc. Ma guardino, ma vedano, ma pensino come è calzato il 5° Alpini! Ma Salandra, ma quello scemo balbuziente d'un re, ma quei duchi e quei deputati che vanno 'a veder le trincee', domandino conto a noi, a me, del come sono calzati i miei uomini: e mi vedrebbe il re, mi vedrebbe Salandra uscir dai gangheri e farmi mettere agli arresti in fortezza: ma parlerei franco e avrei la coscienza tranquilla. Ora tutti declinano la responsabilità: i fornitori ai materiali, i collaudatori ai fornitori, gli ufficiali superiori agli inferiori, attribuiscono la colpa; tutti si levano dal proprio posto quando le responsabilità stringono. Gli Italiani sono tranquilli quando possono persuader sé medesimi di aver fatto una cosa, che in realtà non hanno fatto; il padre che ha speso dieci mila lire per l'educazione del figlio, pensa: 'Ho speso dieci mila lire; certo mio figlio farà bene; perché? perché ho speso dieci mila lire.' E magari il figlio gli muore suicida: e il padre dice allora: 'Oh come?' e non pensa neppure di aver qualche colpa. Così Salandra, così il re, così tutti: fanno le visite al fronte, guardano le cose con gli occhi dei cortigiani: ma non le guardano col proprio occhio, acuto, sospettoso, rabbioso. Il generale Cavaciocchi, che deve essere un perfetto asino, non ha mai fatto una visita al quartiere, non

month's service puts them out of use. This results in total disaster, not just for the exchequer but for the morale of the troops who suffer the shame of this laceration and – in war – the horrors of the freezing cold! So much self-sacrifice in these men, 38 years old and so badly treated! How easily I understand, then, their grumbling, their poor discipline! They bear the real burden of the war, the moral, financial and physical burden, and they are the worst treated. People who shoe soldiers like this – whether through fraud or carelessness – are criminals. If I had seen a shoe factory owner yesterday, I'd have started a fight, before stabbing him to death.

'How now? A rat . . .? A rat! Dead for a ducat, dead!' 'O, I am slain.'

We Italians are too acquiescent to Evil; faced with the causes of our ruin we say: 'O well!', and let things run on. It is not an exaggeration to recognise the necessity of the ultimate sanction under law for these fraudsters, since their crime, as well as defrauding the country, ruins the morale of the Army. I hope that they die of consumption, or hunger, or see their children butchered with axes. Those pregnant cows, those flabby-bellied ministers and senators and big brave generals. I bet they think they have helped their country with their speeches, their visits to the front, their interviews, etc. Let them look, let them see, let them know how the 5th Alpine Regiment is shod! Let Prime Minister Salandra, let that stuttering fool of a king, or those dukes and those politicians who go 'to see the trenches', ask us, ask me, about my men's boots: and the king would see me, Salandra would see me fly off the handle so that they would have to arrest me: but I would speak frankly and would have a clear conscience. Now everyone refuses responsibility: the suppliers blame the materials, the testers blame the suppliers, the senior officers blame the junior officers; everyone leaves their post when responsibility comes calling. Italians are happy when they can persuade themselves that they have done something while in reality they have done no such thing; the father who has spent ten thousand lire on his son's educa-tion, he thinks, 'I've spent ten thousand lire, so of course my son will do well! Why? Because I spent ten thousand lire.' And let's say his son goes and kills himself: so father then says: 'But why?' and does not even think of having done something wrong. Salandra, the king, all of them, they make their visits to the front, looking at things through the eyes of yes-men: but they do not look with their own eyes, sharp, suspicious, furious. General Cavaciocchi, who must be a perfect ass, has never

s'è mai curato di girare per gli alloggiamenti dei soldati. Asini, asini, buoi grassi, pezzi da grand hotel, avana, bagni; ma non guerrieri, non pensatori, non ideatori, non costruttori; incapaci d'osservazione e d'analisi, ignoranti di cose psicologiche, inabili alla sintesi; scrivono nei loro manuali che il morale delle truppe è la prima cosa, e poi dimenticano le proprie conclusioni.

Edolo, 25 settembre 1915

È stata questa una giornata tragica: una di quelle giornate in cui mi domando perché vivo, e se non sarebbe meglio farmi scoppiar la testa con un colpo di revolver: subito, naturalmente, il pensiero di mia madre insorge nella mia anima, il pensiero dei miei amati fratelli, e comincia una vicenda di torture, di immaginazioni dolorose, di pensieri tetri. Ora è subentrato un senso di rassegnazione amara, che l'immagine di mia madre e de' miei fratelli cambia a quando a quando in dolore. Li vedo con me, col povero papà, in una mattina di Pasqua, in Brianza: entusiasmarsi alla ricerca delle màmmole, giubilare di un folto di fiori. Che mi farebbe ora un mazzo di violette? Non sarei capace neppure di arrestarvi lo sguardo. Penso al mio Enrico che combatterà, alla mamma e alla Clara a casa sole, a me, debole come il più debole degli uomini, gettato da una vita orribilmente tormentata a questi giorni di squallore spirituale. È strano come i giorni dell'infanzia, dell'adolescenza, ritornano a torturami con visioni di felicità perduta, specie con il viso de' miei cari: e come penso con insistenza alla Brianza, più che a Milano; ora vedo la ferrovia che giunge a Erba e le strade buie presso Longone, e i campi, nella pioggia autunnale: penso soprattutto alla mamma. [Mamma . . . madre . . .]

Ora, come in un improvviso cortocircuito della mente, riaffioreranno alcuni versi della scena fra Amleto e sua madre . . .

AMLETO

. . . E ora, madre, che c'è?

MADRE

Amleto, tu hai molto offeso tuo padre.

AMLETO

Madre, voi avete molto offeso mio padre.

visited the quarters, has never bothered to inspect the soldier's lodgings. Asses, asses, big fat oxen, grand hotel ninnies, Havana-smokers, water-takers; but not warriors, not thinkers, not inventors, not builders; incapable of observation and analysis, ignorant of psychology, incapable of synthesis; they write in their handbooks that the morale of the troops is the first priority, and then they forget their own conclusions.

Edolo, 25th September 1915

It has been a tragic day: one of those days when I wonder why I am alive, and whether it would be better to blow my head off with a revolver: straight away, of course, the thought of my mother rises up in my soul, the thought of my beloved siblings, and a torturous ordeal begins, of painful imaginings, dismal thoughts. A sense of bitter resignation takes over, and the image of my mother and my siblings changes it now and again into pain. I see them with me, with my poor father, on an Easter morning, in Brianza: joyfully in search of violets, delighting in a clump of flowers. What use would a bunch of violets be to me now? I wouldn't be able to even look at them. I think of my Enrico, who will go to fight, of mother and of Clara at home alone, of me, weak as the weakest of men, thrown by a horribly tormented life into these days of spiritual squalor. It's strange how the days of childhood, adolescence, return to torture me with visions of lost happiness, especially the faces of my loved ones: and how I keep thinking of Brianza, rather than of Milan, and now I see the railway line to Erba and the dark country roads around Longone, and the fields, in the autumn rain: I am thinking above all of Mother [Mum . . .].

Now, in a sudden short circuit of the mind, some verses from the scene between Hamlet and his mother float up to the surface . . .

HAMLET

Now, mother, what's the matter?

MOTHER

Hamlet, thou hast thy father much offended.

HAMLET

Mother, you have my father much offended.

MADRE

Via, via, voi rispondete stravagantemente.

AMLETO

Andate, andate, voi domandate malignamente.
. . . Non vedete niente?!

MADRE

Niente! Vedo soltanto quel che c'è.

AMLETO

Né udiste niente?

MADRE

No! Se non noi due.

AMLETO

Ma guardate un po' là, che si allontana . . . Mio padre (papà!) nei suoi abiti come da vivo! Guardate dov'è: laggiù! Ancora! Su l'uscire . . .

A questo punto il Nostro riprenderà il brano successivo del suo diario rievocato, ma per un attimo sarà come se fosse sempre Amleto a parlare nel suo delirio concitato, in una impercettibile dissolvenza fra le parole del Bardo e quelle del Lombardo . . .

Da casa nessuna notizia, nessuna da Enrico! Dalla guerra brutte notizie, dei Balcani dico! Tristezza su tutta la linea, buio assoluto quanto al futuro, desiderio di scomparire, di finire. Nessun affetto presente, solo aridità negli altri. Solitudine nelle ore di raccoglimento, tetra e squallida. La volontà non è temprata bene; onde il mio spirito non sa procacciarsi quella serenità e quella calma che sono l'edificio più nobile cui possa pervenire un uomo. Ondeggio tra un desiderio e l'altro; tra un sogno e l'altro. Certo, per chi ama come amo io la patria, è difficile essere calmi, sereni, vedendo che le cose non vanno come dovrebbero andare. Gli egoismi schifosi, i furti, le pigrizie, le viltà che si commettono nell'orga-nizzazione militare, la svogliatezza e l'inettitudine di molti, prostrano, deludono, attristano, avvelenano anche i buoni, anche i migliori, anche i più forti: figuriamoci me! Molte volte cerco di non vedere, di non sentire, di non parlare, per non soffrir troppo.

MOTHER

Come, come, you answer with an idle tongue.

HAMLET

Go, go, you question with a wicked tongue.
. . . Do you see nothing there?

MOTHER

Nothing at all, yet all that is I see.

HAMLET

Nor did you nothing hear?

MOTHER

No, nothing but ourselves.

HAMLET

Why, look you there. Look, how it steals away. My father (dad!), in his
habit as he lived. Look, where he goes even now out at the portal . . .

*At this point our hero resumes the next entry of his remembered diary,
but for a moment it will be as if Hamlet were still talking in his agitated
delirium, in a strange crossfade between the words of the Bard and those
of the Gran Lombardo . . .*

No news from home, nothing from Enrico! Bad news from the war,
from the Balkans, I mean! Sadness all down the line, complete darkness
as to the future, the desire to disappear, to finish. No family and friends
around, only sterility in others. Solitude in the hours of rest, gloomy and
miserable solitude. The will is not well tempered, hence my spirit cannot
procure for itself the serenity and calm that are the most noble projects
of a man. I flit from one desire to another, from one dream to another.
Of course, for those who love as I love my country, it is difficult to be
calm, serene, seeing that things are not going the way they should. The
disgusting egotism, the thefts, the laziness, the cowardice that is committed in the military; the slackness and the ineptitude of many, bring
down, disappoint, sadden, poison even the good ones, even the best,
even the strongest, never mind me! Many times I try not to see, not to
hear, not to speak, so as not to suffer too much.

Prima di riprendere a riferire con rinnovato slancio i diari del 1916, il nostro 'Hamlet di via Blumenstihl' – balzato all'interno del suo spazio amletico, debitamente illuminato – si rivolgerà ora al pubblico per chiarire il suo pensiero, dicendo:

L'anima del Principe di Danimarca giganteggia . . . In lui non si contorce il dubbio: chi ha mai inventato questa scemenza?! Si palesa invece un dibattito!

(Ripetuto due volte, sempre più risentito.)

ANNO 1916 – Diario del Gaddus – Sempre in culo a Cecco Beppo!

Giorno 22 giugno 1916
In trincea, sulla falda orientale del piccolo rilievo roccioso a sud di Monte Magnaboschi.

Le nostre fanterie sono buone: il soldato italiano è pigro, specie il meridionale: è sporchetto per necessità, come il nemico, ma anche per incuria: provvede ai bisogni del corpo nelle vicinanze della trincea, riempiendo di merda tutto il terreno: non si cura di creare un unico cesso; ma fa della linea tutto un cesso; tiene male il fucile che è sporco e talora arrugginito; disperde le munizioni e gli strumenti da zappatore (quali fatiche devo durare io per radunare i miei picconi e badili!); dormicchia durante il giorno, mentre potrebbe rafforzare la linea; in compenso però è paziente, sobrio, generoso, buono, soccorrevole, coraggioso, e impetuoso nell'attacco. Non si ha idea di che spaventosa violenza fu il bombardamento sostenuto *allo scoperto* dai reggimenti 157° e 158° che mantennero quasi tutta la linea, con coraggio eroico. E quanto è grande il coraggio che occorre a rimaner fermi sotto il mostruoso fuoco d'artiglieria! Ne so ora qualche cosa.

21 luglio 1916
Semper in eodem loco.
Aggrappati al pendio, in tane semisotterranee, i miei soldati passano il loro tempo sul suolo, come porci in letargo: dimagrano per questa vita orizzontale e si infiacchiscono. Ma la ragione determinante della mia attuale prostrazione è un'antica, intrinseca qualità del mio spirito, per cui il pasticcio e il disordine mi annientano. Io non posso fare qualcosa, sia pure leggere un romanzo, se intorno a me non v'è ordine. Ho qui tanta roba da vivere come un signore: macchina fotografica, liquori, oggetti da toilette, biancheria: e non mi lavo mai neppure le mani e non

Before resuming the entries from his diaries of 1916 with renewed vigour, our 'Hamlet of Via Blumenstihl' – having jumped into his Hamletian space, suitably lit up – will turn now to the public, to clarify his thinking and say:

The soul of the Prince of Denmark looms . . . There is no doubt in him. Who invented this nonsense? Instead there arises a debate!

(Uttered twice, with increasing resentment.)

YEAR 1916 – The Diary of Gaddus – Up Yours, Franz Josef!

22nd June

In the trenches on the eastern slopes of the small rocky hill south of Monte Magnaboschi.

Our infantry are good: the Italian soldier is lazy, especially the Southerner: he is a little dirty out of necessity, just like the enemy, but also out of negligence: he does his business close to the trench, filling the whole terrain with shit: he doesn't bother to dig a single shithole, but makes the whole line a shithole; he doesn't look after his gun which is dirty and sometimes rusty; he leaves ammunition and his sapper's tools (what hardships I have to endure to gather together my picks and shovels!); he dozes during the day, while he could be strengthening the line; to make up for it, however, he is patient, sober, generous, good, helpful, brave and impetuous in attack. You have no idea how frighteningly violent was the bombardment sustained *in the open* by the 157th and 158th regiments, who maintained almost the entire line with heroic courage. And how much courage it takes to hold fast under the monstrous fire of enemy artillery! I now know something of it.

21st July 1916
Semper in eodem loco.

Clinging to the slope, in semi-underground burrows, my soldiers spend their time on the ground, like pigs in hibernation: they sicken and lose weight due to this horizontal life. But the main reason for my current prostration is an ancient, inherent quality of my spirit, which means that mess and disorder completely unnerve me. I can't do anything, even read a novel, if things around me aren't orderly. I have enough stuff for me here to live like a gentleman: camera, liqueurs, toiletries, linen: and I don't even wash my hands and never even sip my grappa so as not to

bevo neppure un sorso di grappa per non scomporre la disposizione della catinella di gomma e degli altri oggetti disposti sul fondo d'una cassa di legno, da birra. Io che mi sono immerso con gioia nelle bufere di neve sull'Adamello, perché esse bufere erano nell'ordine naturale delle cose e io in loro ero al mio posto, io sono atterrito al pensiero che il soffitto del mio abituro sgocciola sulle mie gambe: perché quella porca ruffiana acqua lì è fuor di luogo, non dovrebbe esserci: perché lo scopo del baracchino è appunto quello di ripararmi dalle fucilate e dalla pioggia. Sicché, per non morir nevrastenico, mi dò alla apatia. Scrivo lettere e bestemmio le mosche, altra fra le più puttane troie scrofe merdose porche ladre e boje forme del creato. Quale impressione, quanto dolore e orrore la fine del povero Cesare Battisti!

L'altro giorno invece, dopo redatto il mio giornale, passò per le nostre posizioni il capitano De Castiglioni del 5° Alpini. Il tono del superiore con cui mi accolse e mi porse la mano venne rapidamente trasformandosi in gentile cordialità quando gli dissi il mio nome, il mio stato di servizio, i miei titoli di studio e la mia origine milanese. Appena io ebbi fatto il mio nome, rimase un po' sopra pensiero: poi, levandosi di bocca il filo d'erba che c'era, e facendo dei moti lievi con la spalla come usava il povero papà, mi chiese appunto: 'lei è di Milano?' Alla mia risposta: 'Signor sì', mi domandò se ero fratello ecc. ecc., come dissi. A un certo punto si volse per congedarci: credendo volesse congedare me pure, mi misi sull'attenti e salutai. Ma egli mi disse: 'no, no lei Gadda viene con me'. E, come fummo soli, di nuovo si informò di me, de' miei studi, di mio fratello, e mi disse di salutarlo. Che uomo! Parlando di mio fratello esclamò: 'Sa che lo faremo presto tenente?' Io, che sono un ardito-impacciato, un petulante-timido, avanzai la domanda se potessi sperare la promozione anche per me: alla qual domanda non degnò neppure di rispondere, lasciandomi avvilito. Mi lasciò, con minore effusione di quella con cui mi aveva accolto: quasi che la mia persona lo avesse deluso, dopo avermi sentito parlare. Con una voce che mi parve avere una lieve intonazione di tristezza e di severità mi disse, stringendomi la mano: 'Addio Gadda, e in gamba, neh! Mi saluti tanto suo fratello'.

Adesso, o Italiani di tutti i tempi e di tutti i luoghi, che avete fatto della patria un inferno per i vostri litigi personali, per le discordie uso La Marmora e Cialdini (che il demonio li copra di sterco: anime schifose), per i veleni, le bizze, le invidie, dall'epoca dei Comuni a questa parte: adesso ditemi: appartengo io alla vostra razza? So vincere la mia ragion

disturb the layout of my rubber basin and the other items arranged in the bottom of a wooden beer crate. To think that I immersed myself with joy in the snowstorms on the Adamello, because these snowstorms were in the natural order of things and I, in them, was in my place, yet I am terrified at the thought that the ceiling of my hovel leaks on my legs: because here that bloody bastard water is out of place, it shouldn't be here: because the purpose of the shack is precisely to shelter me from gunfire and rain. Therefore, in order not to die a nervous wreck, I surrender to apathy. I write letters and swear at flies, another of the most filthy slut whore bitch pig thief bastard forms of creation. What a shocking, what a chilling, horrible and painful end poor Cesare Battisti came to!

The other day, however, after I had written in my journal, Captain De Castiglioni of the 5th Alpini passed by. The businesslike tone with which he welcomed me and offered me his hand quickly turned into warm-heartedness when I told him my name, my service record, my qualifications and my Milanese origins. As soon as I had given my name, he stood a moment in thought: then, taking from his mouth the piece of grass that was there, and making slight movements with his shoulder, just like my poor dad used to, he asked, 'Are you from Milan?' At my reply – 'Sir, yes Sir' – he asked me if I was the brother of, etc. etc., and I said I was. At one point he turned to dismiss us, and, believing he would dismiss me as well, I stood to attention and saluted. But he said, 'No, no, Gadda. Come with me'. And, as soon as we were alone, he asked me more questions, about my studies, about my brother, and told me to say hello to him. What a man! While talking about my brother he exclaimed: 'Did you know we will soon make him a lieutenant?' I, being boldly clumsy and petulantly shy, dared to raise the question of whether I could hope for promotion as well, a question he did not deem worthy of an answer, leaving me dejected. He left me with less warmth than he had met me with: almost as if he was disappointed by me, having heard me speak. With a voice that seemed to have a slight tone of sadness and severity, he told me, shaking my hand: 'Goodbye, Gadda, and Good Luck, what! Give my best to your brother'.

Now, all you Italians of all times and all places, who made of your country a hellhole for your personal battles, for your petty disagreements like La Marmora and Cialdini (I hope that the devil covers them with crap: bastard souls), for your poisons, your tantrums, your envies, from the time of the city states to today: now, tell me: do I belong to

personale con la ragione dell'interesse del servizio e della concordia, oppur no? Rispondo al glorioso motto dei Gesuiti, che dovrebbe essere il motto di ogni soldato, come anche prescrive il regolamento di disciplina ('la persona del soldato deve scomparire dinanzi alle esigenze del servizio, della patria'), rispondo al glorioso motto: '*Perinde ac cadaver*'?

[Cos'è più nobile?] . . . Cogliere il bacio bugiardo della Parvenza, coricarsi con lei sullo strame, respirare il suo fiato, bevere giù dentro l'anima il suo rutto e il suo lezzo di meretrice? O invece attuffarla nella rancura e nello spregio come in una pozza di scrementi, e negare, negare . . .?

> The time is out of joint. O cursed spite,
> That ever I was born to set it right!

> Il secolo è fuori dai cardini. Maledetto destino
> che io sia nato per rimetterlo in sesto!

Le luci dissolvono al buio lentamente. Musica. Un brano dal Pierrot lunaire *di Arnold Schönberg risuona beffardo nell'aria.*

your race? Do I not overcome my own personal motives in the interests of the service and national harmony? Do I not live according to the glorious motto of the Jesuits, which should be the motto of every soldier, as the Values and Standards state ('This means putting the needs of the mission and of the team before personal interests') – do I not follow the glorious motto: '*Perinde ac cadaver*'?

[What is nobler?] . . . To seize the lying kiss of Appearance, to lie with her on the straw, to breathe her breath, to drink deep into the soul her belch and strumpet's stench? Or rather to plunge her into rancour and contempt as into a well of excrement, and to deny, deny . . .?

> The time is out of joint. O cursed spite,
> That ever I was born to set it right!

The lights slowly dim. Music. A passage from Arnold Schönberg's Pierrot Lunaire *mockingly fills the air.*

3. La cattura e il ritorno

Ora il nostro 'Amleto Pirobutirro' si accinge a leggere l'ultimo capitolo della sua triste istoria . . . (All'inizio sarà sul fondo della scena, seduto di spalle.)

I particolari della battaglia dell'Isonzo e della mia cattura, raccolti pro-memoria, in caso di accuse. (Narrazione per uso personale, scrupolosamente veridica.) Non ho inchiostro.

Così marciando avvistammo sul bellissimo stradale della sponda opposta una fila di soldati neri, che provenivano da Caporetto, preceduti da alcuni a cavallo; il cuore mi s'allargò pensando che fossero nostri rincalzi, e al momento quell'uniforme nera mi fece pensare (che stupido) ai bersaglieri; non pensavo che questi, in combattimento, hanno l'uniforme grigio verde. Poco dopo il crepitio d'una mitragliatrice e qualche colpo di fucile: cominciai allora a temere e intravedere la verità: 'i Tedeschi saliti da Tolmino! Stanno per circondarci'. Intravidi ormai il pericolo della prigionia, e affrettai il passo, per raggiungere Cola, la passerella, non so che. L'ansia diveniva spasmodica. Disperavo di trovar Cola, quando ci sentimmo chiamare, da poco sotto il ciglione. 'Gadda!' 'Cola' 'eh?' 'Siamo qui'. Mi ricordo esattamente che appena lo vidi gli chiesi: 'che è?' '*Sono loro, siamo perduti*', mi rispose. 'Sono loro? Ma è possibile?' e non seppi dir altro, né far altro che piangere. 'Ah! è orribile, è orribile', esclamò Cola (parole precise), 'Più che se fosse morto mio padre. Siamo finiti'.

I soldati s'erano raccolti intorno a noi. Io e Cola pensammo quindi ormai inutile il prolungare le nostre speranze; sarebbe stato puerile. De Candido uscì con un fazzoletto bianco, mentre io e Raineri guastavamo le armi della mia sezione, asportandone e disperdendone la culatta mobile, il percussore e altri pezzi. Che dolore, che umiliazione, che pianto nell'anima anche in quest'atto ormai inevitabile. Erano le 13.20 del 25 ottobre 1917; facemmo nel prato l'ultima adunata, l'ultima

3. The capture and return

Now our 'Hamlet Pirobutirro' is about to read the last chapter of his sad story . . . (At first, he will be at the back of the stage, with his back to the audience.)

The details of the Battle of the Isonzo and of my capture, gathered as a memorandum, in case of accusations. (Account for personal use, meticulously truthful.) I have no ink.

So. Marching, we saw, on the beautiful road on the opposite bank a line of black-uniformed soldiers, coming from Caporetto, preceded by some on horseback. My heart swelled with joy, thinking they were our reinforcements, and at that moment that black uniform made me think (idiot) of the bersaglieri. I wasn't thinking that they, in action, wear a grey-green combat uniform. Shortly after, the crackle of a machine gun and some rifle fire: I then began to fear and face the truth: 'Germans come up from Tolmino! They're going to surround us'. I now foresaw the danger of imprisonment, and quickened my pace to reach Cola, the jetty, I don't know what. My anxiety turned to panic. I had nearly despaired of finding Cola, when we heard a voice call, just below the ridge. 'Gadda!' 'Cola!' 'Eh?' 'Here we are!' I remember exactly that as soon as I saw him, I asked him: 'What's going on?' *'It's them, we're done for'*, he answered. 'It's them? Can it be?' And I could not say more, nor do anything but cry. 'Ah! It's horrible, it's horrible', Cola said (his exact words). 'This is worse than if my father died. We're finished'.
    The soldiers had gathered around us. Cola and I thought it then useless to prolong our hopes; it would have been childish. De Candido went out with a white handkerchief, while Raineri and I put my section's weapons out of action, removing and throwing away the sliding breeches, the firing pins and other pieces. How painful, how humiliating: what tears the soul shed in this inevitable action! It was 13.20 on 25th October 1917; we had the last muster in the meadow, the last call.

chiamata. Col pianto negli occhi e nel cuore mi congedai da ciascuno, stringendo a tutti la mano. Finiva così la nostra vita di soldati e di bravi soldati, finivano i sogni più belli, le speranze più generose dell'adolescenza: con la visione della patria straziata, con la nostra vergogna di vinti iniziammo il calvario della dura prigionia, della fame, dei maltrattamenti, della miseria, del sudiciume. Ma ciò fa parte di un altro capitolo della mia povera vita, e questo martirio non ha alcun interesse per gli altri. Finito di scrivere, in Rastatt, il 10 dicembre 1917.

ANNO 1919

Giorno 3 gennaio
Casello ferroviario presso la piccola stazione di Pfiffligheim Worms. Stanza da pranzo del casellante. Ore 18.30.

Il campo di prigionia di Celle-Lager fu interamente sgomberato la mattinata del primo gennaio. Notte serena e fredda; non si dormì; attesa nel vento gelato, a Scheuen. Saliamo in treno congelati. Io sono con Betti, Sciaccaluga, Meucci, Rossetti, Battiato, Mazzacchera, San Filippo; otto nel posto da sei. Pigiati l'un contro l'altro tra l'ingombro del bagaglio leggero, coi finestrini rotti che ostruiamo mediante salviette e pezze, per rompere al vento e al gelo il loro passo maledetto, facciamo un viaggio ben gramo, consolato solo da qualche risata, dalla gioia latente e diffusa del rimpatrio, e dalle scatolette della Croce Rossa Inglese. Il treno ci esaspera per la sua lentezza; percorre a passo d'uomo e di cavallo zoppo, con soste enormi nelle stazioni, la linea Hannover-Hildesheim-Bebra; Francoforte-Worms.

Noto soltanto alcune date, nell'orrore.

– Partenza improvvisa da Lione la sera del 12. Camionnati alla stazione di Bottreaux, ci fanno lasciare a Oullins tutto il bagaglio; Grenoble; salgono gli altri. Giorno 13 gennaio: tempo sereno, ma grande tristezza in me e scarsa emotività anche al rivedere le Alpi. Moncenisio: Italia! È la sera del 13: stellato freddo e grande tristezza.
– Torino: ore 21.30 dello stesso 13 gennaio: i Gallone e i Simonetta mi dicono che i miei stanno tutti bene, anche Enrico. In me tristezza. Mi fanno mangiare al 'Lagrange': Champagne agli 'eroici reduci'. Tristezza. Lettera di Clara consegnatami da Frattini: vogliono ch'io vada a Milano. Clara e mamma erano state ad incontrarmi a

With tears in my eyes and my heart I took my leave of each of the men, shaking every one by the hand. Thus ended our lives as soldiers and good soldiers, thus ended our most beautiful dreams, the best hopes of our adolescence: with the vision of our country torn apart, in our shame as losers, we began the Calvary of hard imprisonment, hunger, abuse, poverty, filth. But all this is part of another chapter of my pitiable life, and this martyrdom contains nothing of interest for others. Journal closed, in Rastatt, 10th December 1917.

YEAR 1919

3rd January

A railway cottage near the small station of Pfiffligheim, Worms. The crossing keeper's front room – 18.30.

The prison camp in Cellelager was entirely vacated on the morning of 1st January. The night was cold and clear, no one slept; we waited in the icy wind, in Scheuen. We climb, frozen, onto the train. I'm with Betti, Sciaccaluga, Meucci, Rossetti, Battiato, Mazzacchera, San Filippo, eight of us in six seats. Pressed against each other between the items of light baggage, with broken windows that we close up with rags and hand-kerchiefs to stop the cursed wind and chill from coming in, we travel dismally, comforted only by a few laughs, the latent and diffused joy of homecoming, and the British Red Cross tins. The train exasperates us with its slowness; it travels at walking pace, like a lame horse, with huge stops in the stations, on the Hannover–Hildesheim–Bebra, Frankfurt–Worms line.

I jot down just a few dates, in the horror.

– Sudden departure from Lyon on the evening of the 12th. Trucked to the station at Bottreaux, we are made to leave all the baggage at Oullins; others get on at Grenoble. 13th January. A clear day, but there's a great sadness in me, and I'm hardly even happy to see the Alps. Moncenisio: Italy! It is the evening of the 13th: starry cold night and great sadness.
– Turin: 21.30 on the same day: the Gallone and the Simonetta families tell me that my folks are all fine, Enrico as well. In me, sadness. They take me to dinner at the 'Lagrange': champagne toast to the 'return-ing heroes'. Sadness. A letter from Clara is given to me by Frattini: they want me to go to Milan. Clara and Mamma went to meet me

Domodossola, due volte! Freddo, disturbo, pena, immenso amore. Tristezza anche per ciò.

– Parto a mezzanotte per Milano, con la tradotta; sto male di nervi, sono stanchissimo e triste. Lugubre viaggio. Direi che presentissi! La patria vuota. Alle 7 circa arrivo in carrozzella a casa. È buio. Busso in portineria; su, suono il campanello. MAMMA, MAMMA; e Clara. Erano a letto; vennero ad aprirmi, ci abbracciamo tanto! Poi seguo la mamma, che s'è rimessa a letto, l'abbraccio nuovamente. 'Ed Enrico dov'è, come sta Enrico?' Mi risponde piangendo la mamma: 'Enrico è andato di qua, di là . . .' La tragica orribile vita. Non voglio più scrivere; ricordo troppo. Automatismo esteriore e senso della mia stessa morte: speriamo passi presto tutta la vita. Condizioni morali e mentali disastrose: Caporetto, gli aeroplani, Enrico, immaginazioni demenziali. È troppo, è troppo.

La mia vita è inutile, è quella d'un automa sopravvissuto a stesso, che fa per inerzia alcune cose senza amore né fede. Lavorerò mediocremente e farò alcune altre bestialità. Sarò ancora cattivo per debolezza, ancora egoista per stanchezza, e bruto per abulia, e finirò la mia torbida vita nell'antica palude dell'indolenza che ha avvelenato il mio crescere mutando le possibilità dell'azione in vani, sterili sogni. Non noterò più nulla, poiché nulla di me è degno di ricordo anche davanti a me solo. Finisco così questo libro di note.

Terminata la rievocazione dei diari di guerra e di prigionia, acquisita coscienza della propria ferita, il nostro Amleto giura, a se stesso, i suoi nuovi 'segreti' propositi . . .

Ci son più cose in cielo e in terra, Orazio che nei sogni del tuo filosofare. Di nuovo qui: che mai – (e Dio vi assista) per quanto in modo strano io mi conduca (può darsi mi convenga d'ora in poi di comportarmi a modo di buffone) – mai, a vedermi, vi sfugga di dire (intrecciando così le braccia o scotendo così la testa) qualche frase equivoca come 'Saprei' o 'Potrei se volessi' 'Se si parlasse . . .' 'Ce n'è che potrebbero' come per suggerire che qualcosa di me sapete. Ora giurate questo. E quando v'è mestieri, Dio v'assista.

at Domodossola, twice! Cold, anxiety, pain, immense love. Sadness because of that as well.

– I'm leaving at midnight for Milan, with the transit. I'm sick with nerves; I'm really tired and sad. Dismal journey. It was like a premonition! The empty motherland. I arrive home in a cab at about 7. It's dark. I knock at the porter's lodge; I go up, ring the bell. MAMMA, MAMMA; and Clara. They were in bed; they come to the door, we embrace for a long time! Then I follow my mother, who went back to bed, and I embrace her again. 'And where is Enrico, how's Enrico?' Mamma answers me, crying: 'Enrico has gone here, there . . .' Tragic, horrible life. I don't want to write any more, I remember too much. On the outside I am an automaton, and I feel I have died my own death: let's hope my life will pass quickly. Disastrous moral and mental conditions: Caporetto, aeroplanes, Enrico, demented imaginings. It's too much, too much.

My life is useless. It's that of an automaton survivor of himself, who, through inertia, does this and that without love or faith. I will work in mediocrity, and I will do some uselessness or other. I will be nasty due to weakness, selfish due to tiredness and brutish due to apathy, and I will end my troubled life in the old swamp of indolence that has poisoned my growth, mutating the possibilities for action into vain, sterile dreams. I will no longer write anything down, because nothing in me is worthy of being remembered, even if only by myself. Here ends my notebook.

The re-enactment of the diaries of war and imprisonment has ended. Having gained awareness of his own pain, our Hamlet swears, to himself, to fulfil his new 'secret' intentions . . .

There are more things in heaven and earth, Horatio, than are dreamt of in your philosophy. But come, here, as before, never, so help you mercy, how strange or odd soe'er I bear myself – as I perchance hereafter shall think meet to put an antic disposition on – that you at such time seeing me never shall, with arms encumbered thus, or this headshake, or by pronouncing of some doubtful phrase as 'Well, we know' or 'We could an if we would', or 'If we list to speak', or 'There be, an if they might', or such ambiguous giving out, to note that you know aught of me – this not to do, so grace and mercy at your most need help you, swear.

Parte una terrificante canzonetta razzista di epoca fascista, cui farà seguito una breve pantomima tragicomica del Nostro. Il dado è tratto: sparire dietro una lingua fuori dall'ordinario, scatenando il suo lessico fantasmagorico, sarà il suo nuovo modo di comunicare col mondo. Fingere, come il Principe di Danimarca, di essere affetto da una particolare forma di follia sarà l'unico modo per sopportare la sua morte in vita. E il suo primo gesto alla Yorick (il buffone di corte della tragedia shakespeariana) sarà una violenta invettiva contro il delirio narcisistico e autoerotico del Tiranno, espressa in un finto fiorentino cinquecentesco . . .

Cue a racist song from the fascist era, which will be followed by a short tragi-comic performance given by our hero. The die has been cast: from now on he will communicate with the world from behind a screen of extraordinary language, through which he unleashes his phantasmagoric vocabulary. Like the Prince of Denmark, only by feigning a particular form of madness can he tolerate his living death. His first 'Yorick' gesture will be a violent invective against the narcissistic and autoerotic delusions of the Duce, expressed in a fake sixteenth-century Florentine idiom . . .

4. Eros e Priapo: da furore a cenere

È ovvio che l'aspirante tiranno o il τύραννος si volga preferentemente agli omini e a' giovani, i quali, adeguatamente insigniti di coltello, possono venir promossi a strumenti precipui della sua birbonata. Dovendo predisporre la tirannia con gli scherani e coi complici, egli cerca, seduce, corrompe, assolda, inquadra scherani maschi e associati maschi nelle milizie, negli uffici, e li sparge con orecchio triplo di spia in mezzo al pòpplo. Senonché il Poffarbacco si preoccupò de le femine. La sua esibita ed esibenda maschilità, sovreccitata da stimolo insano lo sospingeva a rivolgersi ancora alle femine che lo incupivano nel desiderio. E avvertito della importanza che le donne possono avere nell''organico' della famiglia e della società, col suo fiuto di furbo di provincia sente che potrà tirare un qualche profitto dando a bere a le grulle che talvolta le sono ch'esse pure hanno senso e capacità politica, talché poi le donne gli vanno mugolando d'attorno col pretesto del comune amore per il pòpplo, in realtà sospinte da una certa lor ghiottoneria ammirativa per il virulento babbeo che regala d'amoroso guiderdone le amiche, ma insomma ne tiene a bada la vedovata lubido.

La donna il τύραννος furioso la conobbe e la annasò. Il pavido idolatra del numero e della forza s'avvide che le femine gli potevano raddoppiare il su' numero e la su' maledetta forza. Se cento mastî urlano cento evviva, cento mastî più le cento femine urlano dugento evviva. E siccome la tendenza al proselitismo talamico vige e vale anche nel 'liberato mondo', i cento evviva muliebri hanno forse un valore più sostanziale o almeno più promettente di quello de' mastî. E allora. Ciò che la legislazione umanitaristica dei 'paesi più progrediti' aveva da tempo almanaccato, proposto, sperimentato in fatto e impastocchiato in ragioni, ciò che il socialismo chiedeva e richiedeva da anni, che la medicina suggeriva da secoli, lui l'Estrovertito se lo appropriò in tre mesi. Con quella pronta mimesi ed espedita procedura del furbo che sembra ai gonzi una imitazione del cuore: ed è una imitazione del calcolo. Sovvenire a la donna povera, massime a la lavoratrice nel tempo della

4. Eros and Priapus – from fury to ashes

It is obvious that the aspiring tyrant or τύραννος should turn by preference to men and youths, who, properly endowed with knives, may be
promoted to chief instruments of his pranks. Having to organise his
tyranny through robbers and accomplices, he seeks, seduces, corrupts,
hires, drills his regiment of thugs and associates in his militia, in offices,
and disperses them to serve as snooping spies among the Citizenry.
Except that the Good Grief turned his thoughts to females. His show
of masculinity, so clearly displayed and excited by an insane stimulus,
prompted him to turn, again and again, to the women for whom he felt
a dark desire. And, aware of the importance that women can have in
the matrix of family and society, with his small-town crook's nose for
profit, he makes them believe that even they, feather-heads as they often
are, have some sense and some capacity for politics, so that then the
women go round him moaning with the pretext of their shared love for
the Citizenry, but in reality driven by a certain gluttony of their own,
admiring the virulent fool who rewards his female friends with loving
accolades, but keeps their widowed desire at bay.

The furious τύραννος knew his women all right, knew their smell as
well. The cowardly idolater of number and strength perceived that females
could double his number and his bloody force. If a hundred males scream
out a hundred 'hurrahs', a hundred males plus their hundred females
scream out two hundred 'hurrahs'. And since the tendency to proselytise
within the conjugal chamber exists and is in force also in the 'liberated
world', the hundred womanly 'hurrahs' have perhaps a more substantial
value or at least a more promising one than that of the men fowk. And so.
That which the humanitarian legislation in the 'more advanced countries'
had long puzzled over, proposed, tested in fact and messed up in reason,
that which socialism had repeatedly called for for years, that which medi-
cine had suggested for centuries, he the Mega-Extrovert appropriated for
himself in three months. With a sharpster's prompt mimesis and quick
thinking that to fools seems a picture of emotion: and is instead a picture

gravidanza inoltrata, alimentarla durante l'allattamento: che segna, non meno della gestazione e del puerperio, un lasso di depauperanti fatiche per l'organismo feminino. Alimentare e portare all'asciutto il bambino! Perciò: Maternità e Infanzia.

Premi nuziali d'un qualche migliaretto di lirucce: ad alcuni, si noti, non a tutti (parlo i bisognosi ed i poveri): a quelli di che avea motivo paventare o sperare, a chi bercia ne' raduni 'kuce kuce' 'scandendo i' nnome di Cavolini in un delirio d'amore' a quelli sì: e a quegli altri canavesani o valdostani che no, perché non hanno imparato a delirare e a scandire, come la comanda la Patria del delirio. E poi, a' monti manco v'ha luogo da radunarsi a berciare: e i berci, se pur fussero, se li porta, come festuca di letamaio, il vento del monte.

Questi premi e queste largizioni compromissive eran presentati alle aggiudicatarie madri come dono del kuce, emanati da la bontà propia e da la propia scarsella del kuce (che lui come lui, viceversa, del suo nonavere non avea mollato un centavo). E ogni volta in quel premeditato intento: di instillare nell'animo e nei visceri della donna: che se lei l'aveva trovato quello eccetera eccetera, se tra tutt' e due insieme gli veniva fatto far cigolare il letto eccetera eccetera, tutto codesto sfruconare, e cigolare, e anfanare e sudare dipendeva tutto dal kuce: dal Gran Khan! Ed era lui il motore primo, lui la vis prima ed autoctona, l'empito glorioso che mandava tutta la macchina.

Te tu vedi: la imago del dittatore (Cacchio) la si univa, la si saldava per tal modo, ne la memoria fisica e ne le carni delle Sofronie, al ricordo viscerale del Tauro zefireo. Il kuce, la patria, lo impero etiopico, il carcadè, le verghe littorie, i cannoni protesi della Littorio erano per sempre incorporati, consustanziati e saldati nella protensione dello Zefirino. Così come i duo fili de' duo metalli-coppia si saldano nella coppia termoelettrica. Te tu vedi, ora, i' ggioco? Se fu ben giocato? Incorporare la propia immagine nella vivente sollecitudine di i' ssu' marito, de le femine, talché tutte vi si avvinghiassero assecurate al littorio per l'eternità.

E la carenza di facoltà critiche, l'assoluta incapacità di documentarsi criticamente, che è propria di certe donne oltreché di moltissimi uomini, lasciò aperto il ricettacolo delle loro psico-fiche riceventi. La dedizione

of calculation. To provide for the poor woman, especially the working woman during the later months of pregnancy, to sustain her during breast-feeding: which marks, no less than gestation and postpartum, a period of impoverishing effort for the female body. To feed and nurse the baby dry! Therefore: Motherhood and Infancy.

Wedding premiums of a miserly few thousand lire: to some, note, not all (I mean the needy and the poor), to those whom he had reason to fear or in whom he had hopes – those who cry out 'Doosh-y Doosh-y' at the meetings 'chanting the name of Moo-so-lecny in a delirium of love'. To those, yes, and to those other Piedmontese or residents of the Aosta Valley no, because they have not learned to chant and rave as the Homeland of delirium commands them. Besides, in the mountains, there's not even a place for rallies and yelling: and even if there were yells, the mountain wind would carry them away like straw from the dung-heap.

These premiums, these compromising hand-outs were presented to the designated mothers as a gift of the Doosh-y, as if they emanated from the very own goodness and the very purse of the Doosh-y (when of course, conversely, being him, of his own non-possessions he had contributed not a penny). And always with that premeditated intent: to instil in the soul and loins of the woman that if she had found that so on and so forth, if the two of them happened to make the bed creak, and so on and so forth, all that rubbing and creaking and panting and sweating, were all thanks to the Doosh-y: to the Great Khan! And he was the prime mover, he was the first and autochthonous vigour, the glorious impulse that set the entire machine in motion.

So you see: the imago of the dictator (Unfruitful Shoot) was united, was welded in this way, in the physical memory and in the flesh of the Euphemias, to the visceral memory of the life-bringing Bull. The Doosh-y, the homeland and the Ethiopian Empire, hibiscus tea, the rods of the lictors, the projecting cannons of the Littorio were forever incarnate, consubstantial and welded together in the projection of the pizzle of the Life-Bringer. As two wires of two coupling metals are welded in thermoelectric coupling. Do you get the game now? Wasn't it well played? Embedding his own image in the living tenderness of the husband – the women's husbands – so that they all cling securely to the lictor for eternity.

And the lack of critical faculties, the absolute inability to educate themselves, which is characteristic of certain women and many men besides, left their brain-cunts open and receptive. The childish dedication to the

minorile al super-maschio, al padre, al padrone, accolse e introitò il dogma. Il dogma fallico ossia il fallo dogmatico pervenne a depositare nell'utero di talune poverine lo scodinzolante zoo, il germe della certezza canonica. 'Questo e non altro'. 'Questa è verità santa e tutto il rimanente è bugia' 'La patria lo esige' 'Morte al Tentenna!' Grate al padre, esso padre o padrone divenne il totem della loro idolatria che non ammette disquisizione critica.

Non è dunque stupore le femine l'abbiano così avuto nel fegato, in del fidik, come dicono a Milano. Lui era il genio tutelare della Italia – (qual viceversa ruinò, e la redusse a ceneri ed inusitato schifìo) – lui ne aveva insegnato ad essere vuomini; ché prima di lui eravamo donne, e l'Adamello e 'l Mandrone e il Lèmerle e il Cengio e il Fàiti ci camminammo sopra e per entro sotto il cielo in saette, con animo di donna: lui cavalcatore di cavalli e di femine in gloria: lui sì sì, lui sederone a cavallo, lui bellone, lui mascellone, lui fezzone, lui buccone, stivalone, provolone, maschio maschione cervellone generalone di greca tripla. Questo sognavano, questo talora ti dicevano le fraudate ammiratrici.

Ma lui, da codeste eguagliate a battaglione, lu' icché voleva? Forse averle tutte per sé? Che no, quantunque pazzo. Lu' e' voleva gli facessono i figli, lui dimandava la Italia la rifigliasse otto in otto come la conigliera, da ne cavar figli, figli, figli da mandare a la guerra, guerra, guerra. Per averne ispediti da dissiparli a morire nel mare, nei monti, ne le nevi, ne' deserti, incuorati da la tromba del poeta 'apriti monte – colmati mare – che l'Italia ha da passare', ma senza calze, senza panni, senz'arme perché 'lo spirito vince la materia': e dove è monte e due metri di neve e non calze, né maglie, e scarpe mosce di cartone, tu allora da quella ineluttabile materia del monte ne cavi lo spirito de la nefrite: della pleurite: della polmonite: dell'artrite: e del congelamento. E chirurghi a tagliare.

Ma chi comanda o richiede il sacrificio agli altri, ha da sacrificarsi per primo: il solo generale ammissibile è colui che suda sangue. L'inspirazione di chi chiede altrui la vita per buttarla nelle sue scipionate del cacchio, alla conquista dell'inesistente petrolio e del roseo fiore del carcadè, io non ammetto lui la possa tog/lier su come fece il Pirgopolinice dagli spettacoli e dalle fanfare: non sono le rubeste cosce de' giovini, per quanto un po' pelose, che sfilano con le guide di plotone lungo la riga bianca di Via dell'Impero 'in allineamento perfetto' (fotografi e cineoperatori appostati) a dover inspirare la politica

super-male, the father, the master, welcomed and took in the dogma. The phallic dogma, or the dogmatic phallus came to deposit a wiggling zoo in the uterus of some poor things, the germ of canonical certainty. 'This and nothing else'. 'This is the holy truth and all the rest is a lie'. 'The country demands it. Death to the Hesitator!' Being grateful to the father, as they are, the father or master becomes the totem of their idolatry, which does not allow critical disquisition.

It is therefore no wonder that the women held him in their hearts, in their ventricles, as they say in Milan. He was the guiding genius of Italy (a country that he in fact ruined and reduced to ashes and scraps) – he had taught us to be men; because before he came, we were women, and we walked on top of and inside the Adamello and the Mandrone and the Lèmerle and the Cengio and the Fàiti – the sky filled with thunderbolts – with the hearts of women: he rode horses, and females in glory: he, yes indeed; he, big arse on horseback; he, the handsome; he, the big jaw; he, the big fez-wearer; he, the big-gobbed, booted, big chancer, big macho, big male, big brainy, big general, four-starred general. His defrauded female admirers dreamed of him: they would even tell you so.
   But what did he want from all these women, from this army of women? Maybe he wanted them all for himself? No, surely not. No matter how crazy he was. He wanted them to make sons, he asked Italy to breed, in litters of eight like rabbits, to bear sons, sons, sons to send to war, war, war. To have soldiers to waste: for them to die at sea, in the mountains, in the snow, in deserts, heartened by the poet's trumpeting, 'Open up, mountain – Fill up, sea – Italy must go where she has to be', but with no socks, no clothes, no weapons because 'the spirit triumphs over matter': and where there is mountain and two metres of snow and no socks, no woollens and only lousy cardboard shoes, then, from that ineluctable matter of the mountain, you extract the spirit of nephritis: of pleurisy: of pneumonia: of arthritis: of freezing. And surgeons chopping things off.

But whoever is in charge or demands the sacrifice of others has to sacrifice himself first: the only admissible general is one who sweats blood. The inspiration of a man who asks others to throw their lives away on his bullshit African adventures in the hunt for non-existent oil or the rosy flowers of the hibiscus, cannot be drawn from, as Pyrgopolynices did, from spectacles and fanfares. The robust – if a little hairy – thighs of the young men that file, led by staff sergeants, down the white line of Via dell'Impero 'in perfect array' (photographers and cameramen appropriately stationed) cannot inspire the politics of a nation and its

d'una nazione e le sue costose e indigeste 'conquiste', vaso di terracotta destinato da Dio a viaggiare in compagnia di vasi di ferro. Questo inspirarsi alle cosce, ai calzoncini corti, a' bei deretani mantegneschi degli òmini e de' cavalli, è Eros ginnico e pittorico e se tu vuoi mantegnesco, non Logos politico. Amo il Mantegna degli Eremitani e ammiro il suo crudele vigore (pittorico) e i suoi esecutori di giustizia, ma non provocherei una guerra per procurami la soddisfazione sadica ed omoerotica di buttarvi a morire i figli di quelle a cui si è largito il premio nuziale perché facessono figli: figli, figli, figli, tanti figli, infiniti figli, da mandarli a morire nella guerra, guerra, guerra, guerra, contro i 'delitti delitti delitti della Inghilterra Inghilterra Inghilterra Inghilterra'. Eros arriva al regno di demenza. Eros è ben brutto quando il minimo cavatappi gli sguazza nel liquor.

A questo punto 'il buffone' ridiventerà terribilmente serio, concludendo . . .

Lui non conobbe quelle angosce, quelle vigilie, quelle speranze sacre, quelle preghiere, quel dolore che formarono il solo pane delle anime, negli anni lontani: e né meno la disperata certezza della ruina, e l'alito della tenebra. Quando penso 'amo la mia gente', cioè i poveri esseri che mi precedettero e m'accompagnano e mi seguiranno nel nulla, di certo io non dico frase da teatro, tanto è vero che né meno mai la proferisco sui labbri: né la inserisco in poetici parti che l'è pensiero giù: prigione soltanto dell'anima. E talvolta, sebbene disseccate da tempo le lacrimarie glandule, gli occhi tuttavia mi si velano pensando i sacrifici, i caduti, il giovine spentosi all'entrare appena in quella che doveva essere la vita, spentosi a ventun anno appiè i monti senza ritorno: perché i ciuchi avessero a ragliare di Patria e di Patria – ià, ià . . . ejà, ejà – dentro il sole baggiano della lor gloria. Che fu gloria mentita. *(Piangendo)*

Lo spettacolo è terminato. Riguadagnando la sua consueta 'posizione amletica' (sull'asse delle ascisse e delle ordinate), l'attore – senza più alcuna 'finzione' – prenderà a interrogarsi su ciò che ha appena vissuto sulla scena per più di un'ora. Asciugato il sudore e ripreso il fiato, rivolto al pubblico, quindi dirà . . .

[Ma secondo voi] Non è (un po' . . .) 'mostruoso' che un attore, solo in una finzione, come dire . . .?, in un sogno di passione, possa forzare la sua anima così al suo proprio concetto che per opera di quella tutto il suo volto è impallidito; lacrime ne' suoi occhi, smarrimento nel suo

expensive and indigestible 'conquests', an earthen vessel destined by God to travel alongside iron vessels. This inspiration through thighs, short trousers, the nice Mantegnesque backsides of men and horses, is gymnastic, pictorial and – if you like – Mantegnesque Eros, not political Logos. I love the Mantegnas in the Church of the Eremitani and I admire his cruel vigour (in painting) and his executors of justice, but I wouldn't start a war to enjoy the sadist and homoerotic satisfaction of sending to their deaths the sons of those I had paid a wedding premium to so that they would produce sons: sons, sons, sons, so many sons, an infinity of sons, to send them to death in war, war, war against the 'crimes crimes crimes of England England England England'. Eros lands in the realm of madness. Eros gets seriously ugly when its minimal corkscrew tail plashes about in the muck.

At this point 'the buffoon' becomes terribly serious again, concluding . . .

He did not know the anguish, those vigils, those sacred hopes, those prayers, that pain which provided the only sustenance for the souls, in years gone by: nor did he know the desperate certainty of ruin and the breath of darkness. When I think 'I love my people', the poor creatures who preceded me and accompany me and will follow me into nothingness, I certainly am not play-acting, so much so that I never utter the phrase: nor will it come from me, set down in poetry: it is the prison only of the soul. And sometimes, though my lachrymal glands have long dried out, my eyes cloud, thinking about the sacrifices, the fallen, the young man who died just as he embarked on what should have been his life, killed at twenty-one at the foot of the mountains with no return, so that the donkeys brayed Fatherland, Patria – hee-aa, hee-ah . . . hey-aa, hey-ah – in the idiot sun of their glory. A false glory. (*Crying*)

The show is over. Regaining his usual 'Hamlet' position (on the horizontal axis and the vertical axis), the actor – no longer 'acting' – takes to questioning himself on what he has just experienced for over an hour. Having wiped off the sweat, and having got his breath back, he will tell the audience . . .

[In your opinion] Is it not [a bit] monstrous that this player here, but in a fiction, in a dream of passion, could force his soul so to his own conceit that from her working all his visage wann'd, tears in his eyes, distraction in's aspect, a broken voice, and his whole function suiting with forms to

aspetto, una voce rotta, e tutte le sue funzioni rispondenti nelle forme al suo concetto? E tutto questo per cosa? Per niente? . . . Per Ecuba . . .! [Ma allora] Questa è cosa assai prode, che io . . . figlio d'un caro padre assassinato, spinto a vendicarmi dal cielo e dall'inferno, mi sia, ora, come una puttana, scaricato l'anima con le parole, e mi sia dato a bestemmiare come una vera baldracca, una troia!

[Oppure . . .]

his conceit? And all for nothing? . . . For Hecuba! [But then] this is most brave, that I, the son of a dear father murder'd, prompted to my revenge by heaven and hell, must, like a whore, unpack my heart with words, and fall a-cursing, like a very drab, a scullion!

[Or . . .]

5. Finale

Rompendo definitivamente il 'gioco dello spettacolo', l'attore concluderà il secondo corno del suo ragionamento dicendo . . .

[Oppure . . .] Bè, i crimini della triste màfia e di tutti li 'entusiasmati' a delinquere avendo raggiunto o me' dirò permeato ogni pensabbile forma del pragma, cioè ogni latèbra del sistema italiano (con una 'penetrazione capillare', oh! sì, davvero), è ovvio che tutte le nostre attività conoscitive e le universe funzioni dell'anima debbano intervenire nel giudizio del male, patito e fatto. [?] [E che] Tutti i periti, e d'ogni sorta medici, hanno e aranno discettare sulla maialata. [Perché] L'atto sacrale di conoscenza con che nu' dobbiamo riscattarci prelude la resurrezione se una resurrezione è tentabile da così paventosa macerie.

Vorrei, e sarebbe mio debito, essere al caso d'aver dottrina di psichiatra e di frenologo di studio consumato in Sorbona: da poter indagare e conoscere [ad esempio] con più partita perizia la follia tetra del Marco Aurelio ipocalcico dalle gambe a ìcchese: autoerotòmane affetto da violenza ereditaria. Da giuntarvi, a tanta lezione, un'altra non meno vera circa la ebefrenica avventatezza del contubernio e della coorte pretoria. Ed altra ed altre circa la demenza totale d'un poppolo frenetizzato. Frenologo non essendo, e tanto meno sifolòlogo, farò icché potrò.

[Dunque:] L'io collettivo è guidato ad autodeterminarsi e ad esprimere sé molto più dagli istinti o libidini vitali, cioè in definitiva da Eros, che non da ragione o da ragionata conoscenza. Da un punto di vista scenico, e dunque relativo al sentimento della pluralità (voi dite 'massa'), avviene che la moltitudine ama e idoleggia l'istrione suo e – così come egli è, o par che sia – *lo desidera*. Questo non ovunque, non sempre, ma di certo ove la gora del divenire si ristagna: e dove si impaluda nelle sue giacenze morte la Storia, e la 'evoluzione' del costume.

5. Finale

Making no attempt at all to maintain any sense of 'play', the actor concludes the second part of his argument by saying . . .

[Or . . .] Well, the crimes of the sad mafia and all those 'enthusiasts' of crime having reached or rather permeated every imaginable form of pragma, that is, each recess of the Italian system (with a blanket penetration, oh! yes, really), it is obvious that all our cognitive activities and the universal functions of the soul must intervene in the judgment of evil suffered and evil committed. [?] [And] All the experts and doctors of every sort must and will have to dissect the swinishness. [Because] The sacred act of knowledge with which we have to redeem ourselves is a sign of the resurrection, if a resurrection is possible from such horrendous wreckage.

I would like, and for that I would be much obliged, to be learned in psychiatry and phrenology through study at the Sorbonne: so as to be able to investigate and know [for example] with more expert skill the sombre madness of that hypocalcaemic Marcus Aurelius with his bandy legs: an autoerotic maniac suffering from hereditary violence. And to add to such a lesson another case, no less true, regarding the hebephrenic recklessness of the barracks and the praetorian cohort: and many, many other cases of the total insanity of a delirious populace. Not being a phrenologist, and much less a syphilologist, I will do what I can.

[So:] The collective ego is driven to self-determination and to express itself much more through instincts or vital libidos, that is through Eros, rather than through reason or rational knowledge. From a theatrical point of view, and therefore playing to the feeling of plurality (you say 'the masses'), the crowds love and idolise their Histrionic Ham and – just as he is, or seems to be – *they desire him.* This does not happen everywhere, and not always, but for certain where the millrace of progress gets stagnant: and where history and the 'evolution' of customs become

Ché te t'hai a ritenere un prencipio: gli impulsi creatori e determinatori di storia grossa e' si immettono in nel miracolato suo deflusso per 'quanti d'energia', e non già in un apporto continovo. La storia grossa conosce le sue paludi, le more de' sua processi, i ritorni, i riboboli inani, le stanche pause. In codesti lachi di storia grossa, dove non è chiamata del futuro, ivi Eros ammolla, e più facilmente infracida e bestialmente gavazza.

Ora questo qui, Madonna bona!, non avea manco finito di imparucchiare quattro sue scolaresche certezze, che son qua mè, a fò tutt me a fò tutt mè. Venuto dalla più sciapita semplicità, parolaio da raduno communitosi del più misero bagaglio di frasi fatte, pervenne infine, dopo le sovvenzioni del capitale, e dopo una carriera da spergiuro, a depositare in càtedra il suo deretano da Pirgopolinice smargiasso, cioè sulla cadrèga di Presidente del Consiglio. Pervenne, pervenne.

[Ora] Non sono psichiatra. Ma chiedendomi taluno il mio contributo a quell'atto di conoscenza di che si ragionava pur dianzi, bene, ecco qua.

[Io dico che] Qualunque si affacci alla vita presumendo occupare di sé solo la scena turpissima dell'agorà e istrioneggiarvi per lungo e per largo da gran ciuco, e di pelosissima orecchia, a tanta burbanza sospinto da ismodata autoerotia, quello, da ultimo, tornerà di danno a' suoi e talora a sé medesimo.

[Perché] Il folle narcissico è incapace di analisi psicologiche, non arriva mai a conoscere gli altri: né i suoi, né i nemici, né gli alleati. Perché? Perché in lui tutto viene relato alla erezione perpetua e alla prurigine erubescente dell'Io-minchia, invaghito, affocato, affogato di sé medesimo. E allora gli adulatori sono tenuti per genî: e per commilitoni pronti a morire col padrone, anzi prima di lui facendo scudo del loro petto. (In realtà, appena sentono odor di bruciato se la squagliano.) I non adulatori sono ripudiati come persone sospette ed equivoche. I contraddittori sono *delinquenti* punibili con decine di anni di carcere. I derisori e gli sbeffeggiatori sono da appendere pel collo.

Seconda caratterizzazione aberrante e analoga alla prima è la loro incapacità alla costruzione etica e giuridica: poiché tutto l'ethos si ha da ridurre alla salvaguardia della loro persona, che è persona scenica e non persona gnostica ed etica, e alla titillazione dei loro caporelli, in italiano capezzoli: e all'augumento delle loro prerogative, per quanto arbitrarie o dispotiche, o tutt'e due. Lo jus, per loro, è il turibolo: religio è l'adorazione della loro persona scenica; atto lecito è unicamente

bogged down in its dead stock. You have to remember one principle: the creative and determining impulses of history join its miraculous flow as 'quanta of energy', and not as a continuous outpouring. History knows its swamps, the arrears of its processes, the comebacks, the inane witticisms, the tired pauses. In these backwaters, where the future exerts no pull, there Eros soaks and rots, all the more ready to sink into bestial revelry.

Now this one here, for Pete's sake, had not even finished half-learning a couple of his schoolboy certainties: 'See me? Here, um uh . . . See me? Ah'm awa' tae dae it aw'. Starting from the most insipid simplicity, a rally windbag equipped with the most wretched store of set phrases, he finally arrived, after grants of capital and after a career as a perjurer, to deposit his rabble-rousing bully's backside on the Prime Minister's cathedra. He came, he finally came.

[Now] I'm not a psychiatrist. But if someone were to ask for my contribution to that act of knowing discussed earlier, well, here goes.

[I tell you that] Anyone who appears on the scene and presumes to occupy, all alone, the polluted, defiled public arena and ham it up far and wide like a great ass with the hairiest ears, driven to such arrogance by unrestrained autoeroticism, will, ultimately, be the ruin of his own people and sometimes of himself.

[Because] The crazy narcissist is incapable of psychological analysis, and never comes to know others: whether family, enemies, or allies. Why? Because for him everything is about the perpetual erection and the erubescent itch of the Ego-Cock, infatuated, aflame, drowning in itself. And so flatterers are taken for geniuses, and for fellow soldiers ready to die with their master, or even before him, shielding him with their chests. (In fact, the minute they smell a rat they scurry off.) The non-sycophants are repudiated as being suspect and equivocal. The nay-sayers are *delinquents* punishable with years in prison: the scoffers and the satirists are to be hanged by the neck.

The second aberrant trait, similar to the first, is their incapacity for ethical and legal construction: since all ethos must be reduced to protecting their own persona, and that persona is more of a theatrical projection rather than one based on knowledge and ethics, and to titillating their diddies – in English nipples – and expanding their prerogatives, however arbitrary or despotic, or both. Ius, for them, is the thurible: religio is the adulation of their theatrical persona; lawful conduct is

l'idolatria patita ed esercitata nei loro confronti; crimine è la mancata idolatria.

Altra modalità dell'aberrazione narcisistica è la morbosa tendenza a 'innalzarsi', ad eccellere in forma scenica e talora delittuosa, senza discriminazione etica: senza subordinare l'Io a Dio. L'autofoja, che è l'ismodato culto della propria facciazza, gli induce a credere d'esser davvero necessari e predestinati da Dio alla costruzione e preservazione della società, e che senza loro la palla del mondo l'abbi rotolare in abisso, nella Abyssos primigenia: mentre è vero esattamente il contrario: e cioè senza loro la palla de i' mondo la rotola come al biliardo e che Dio esprime in loro il male dialetticamente residuato dalla non-soluzione dei problemi collettivi: essi sono il residuato male defecato dalla storia, lo sterco del mondo.

Il *contenuto* del pragma narcissico è limitato a quel groppo di porta-menti e di gesti che ponno attuare la relazione (ottica, acustica) con la desiderata platea, che soli possono procurargli l'applauso. Groppo che diviene persona: la è tutta lì la 'persona'. Il Golgota [per dire] non è scena, non è disonor del Golgota degno di lui. Per lui non il legno della croce, ma il cesso di lapislazzuli o il bidet di onice. Esibisce [invece] voci e canti da magnificar l'Io nella voce, nel frastorno. La voce è richiamo sessuale potente e gravita, per così dire, sull'ovaio alle genti. Il folle narcissico e' desidera e brama le carte stampate, per quanto coartate e vane, i giornali magnificanti le su' glorie, e de' sua. Gli stessi annunci funebri, i soffietti pubblicitari se gli è privato uomo titillano la sua lubido narcissica. Morirebbe, 'per andà in sul giornàal'.

Ma la nota dominante del pensiero, della parola e dell'atto è la menzo-gna narcissica. La menzogna narcissica è, nel procedere della storia, quel che è la dissipazione nella vita privata. Consiste nel negare una serie di fatti reali che non tornano graditi a messer 'Io'. La menzogna esce di getto dalla sua anima come dogma irruente, come uno spillo d'acqua da una manichetta de' pompieri sotto pressione. Si sente che nessuna remora, nessuna obiezione potrà fermarla. Lo stesso vediamo fare con resultati pressoché identici, alla isterica o all'ipocondriaco e in genere a quelli che sono smagati da un 'delirio interpretativo' dei fatti reali. (Questo termine è dello psicologo francese Capgras.) Se la isterica menta consapevole o no, è una delle questioni classiche dibattute dalla psicopa-tologia: e io non ho né dottrina né forze né tempo né carte da istruirne a

uniquely equated to idolatry proffered to them and accomplished; crime is the lack of idolatry.

Another mode of narcissistic aberration is the morbid tendency to 'raise oneself up', to excel in theatrical and sometimes criminal form, without ethical discrimination: without subordinating the Ego to God. The auto-erotic itch, which is the unrestrained cult of their ugly faces, convinces them that they are really necessary and predestined by God to construct and preserve society, and that without them the ball of the world would roll into the abyss, the primeval Abyssos: while exactly the opposite is true: that without them the ball of the world rolls like a billiard and through them God expresses the evil that, dialectally, is left behind by the non-solution of collective problems: they are the residual evil def-ecated by history, the dung of the world.

The *content* of narcissistic pragma is confined to that tangle of behaviours and actions that can implement the relationship (optical, acoustic) with the desired audience, which alone can procure applause. A tangle that becomes person: that's the nub of it, the 'person'. Golgotha [so to speak] is not theatre, it is not the dishonour of Golgotha that the narcissist deserves. For him, not the wooden cross, but the lapis lazuli latrine or the onyx bidet. He shows off [instead] with voices and songs to magnify the ego through the voice, in noisy confusion. The voice is a powerful sexual attractor and exerts gravity, so to speak, on the ovary of the people. The narcissistic manic desires and longs for the printed page, however forced and useless, for the newspapers magnifying his glories and his people. Even the death notices, even the private ads, if he is not in the public eye, titillate his narcissistic libido. He would die, 'to get into the papers'.

But the dominant trait, in thought, word and deed, is the narcissistic lie. The narcissistic lie is, in the progress of history, the same as the act of squandering in private life. It consists of negating a series of real facts that do not add up with Mr 'Ego'. The lie bursts out of the soul like impetu-ous dogma, like a jet of water from a fire-hose under pressure. No com-punction, no objection can stop it. We see the same thing, with almost identical results, in individuals who are hysterical or hypochondriac and in general in those confused by an 'interpretive delirium' of the real facts. (This term was coined by the French psychologist Capgras.) Whether the hysterical patient lies consciously or not is one of the classic debates of psychopathology: and I do not have the learning, strength, time or paper to go over the debate for the thousandth time. The narcissistic

questi anni per la millesima volta il dibattito. La menzogna narcissica, la reticenza narcissica, la calunnia narcissica direi, un po' a lume di naso, che pertengono alle zone conscie dell'Io: e pure comportano un che di ineluttabile, di 'fatale', di teso: di biologicamente predeterminato quasi dall'eccessivo esondare di un dato ormone: esse rasentano certi stati di sogno, di utopia folle e felice che da non so quali stupefacenti si procacciano. Uno si crede Cesare perché fa inscrivere il nome Caesar su alcuni sassi. Sogna. Le genti sensate gli ridono in faccia. Allora il malato li fa prendere e li fa carcerare per decine di anni.

SUL PALCO, SUL PODIO, LA MASCHERA DELL'ULTRA ISTRIONE E DEL MIMO, LA FALSA DRAMMATICITÀ DE' RAGLI IN SCENA, I TACCHI TRIPLI DA FAR ECCELLERE LA SU' NANERIA: E NIENT'ALTRO.

FINE

lie, narcissistic reticence, narcissistic slander: as a little rule of thumb, I would say that they belong to the conscious areas of the Ego: and yet there is something of the ineluctable, something 'fatal', something tense about them: something biologically predetermined, almost like the excessive flooding of a given hormone: they border on certain states of dream, of mad, happy utopia brought on by I don't know what kinds of drugs. One man believes he is Caesar because he has the name of Caesar inscribed on a few stones. He's dreaming. Sensible people laugh in his face. Then the madman has them arrested and imprisoned for decades.

ON THE STAGE, ON THE PODIUM, THE MASK OF THE ULTRA HYSTRIONIC HAM AND OF THE MIME, THE FAKE DRAMA OF HIS THEATRICAL BRAY-INGS, TRIPLE HEELS TO EXALT HIS DWARFISHNESS: AND NOTHING ELSE.

THE END

Endnote

Incipit. Opening from *Hamlet*, II, ii, 191–206 ('What are you reading [. . .] method in't'). This is followed by the first extract from Gadda, a passage enti-tled (after Vergil, *Eglogue*, IV, 62) 'Cui non risere parentes'. Originally part of the compositional notes for *La cognizione del dolore*, the fragment was later discarded and not included in Gadda (1963 and 1970) – see Gadda (1987: 527–35).

The diaries. Opening from *Hamlet*, I, v, 98–104 ('Yea, from the table [. . .] yes, by heaven!'), with play, but only in the English, on the common trope of the 'bad apple', which morphs into 'bad pear' from Pirobutirro (*Buttery-pear*), the protagonist's surname in both *La cognizione* and *L'ingegner Gadda va alla guerra*. The entries in this section come from *Giornale di guerra e di prigionia* (Gadda 1955, 1965 – GGP SGF II 431–867). More specifically: SGF II 441 ('The Ministry of War bulletin [. . .] my training'), 443–4 (24th August 1915), 449–50 (28th August 1915), 451 (31st August 1915), 452 (2nd September 1915), 454–5 (7th September 1915), 495 ('Lieutenant Pozzi [. . .] "Geddit?"'), 466–8 (20th September 1915), 470–1 (25th September 1915), 475 ('No news from home [. . .] suffer too much'), 518 ('Year 1916'), 542 (22nd June 1916), 546 ('Our infantry are good [. . .] something of it'), 570–1 ('Semper in eodem loco [. . .] Battisti came to!'), 586–7 ('The other day [. . .] your brother'), 597

('Now, all you [. . .] *ac cadaver?*') – with the exceptions of two further excerpts
from other texts by Gadda: VM SGF I 539 ('The soul of the Prince [. . .] arises a
debate' – from Gadda's review of a 1952 Italian production of *Hamlet*, '*Amleto*
al Teatro Valle') and CdD RR I 703 ('To seize the lying kiss [. . .] deny, deny
. . .?', from the opening of chapter 7 of *Cognizione*, here with more than a hint
of *Hamlet*, III, i, 57, 'Whether 'tis nobler in the mind to suffer', and resulting in
the addition of question marks, which instead were implicit in the Gadda original). The further interpolations from *Hamlet* come from: III, iv, 24–5 ('How
now? A rat . . .? [. . .] I am slain'); III, iv, 8–12, 131–6 ('Now, mother, what's
the matter? [. . .] wicked tongue'; 'Do you see nothing [. . .] out at the portal!');
I, v, 188–9 ('The time is out of joint [. . .] set it right!').

The capture and return. Further diary entries – GGP SGF II 697 ('The details
of the Battle [. . .] no ink'), 733–4 ('So. Marching, we saw [. . .] we're finished'),
734 ('The soldiers had gathered'), 736 ('Cola and I thought [. . .] inevitable
action!'), 737 ('It was 13.20 [. . .] every one by the hand'), 740 ('Thus ended
our lives [. . .] 10th December 1917'), 845 ('Year 1919 [. . .] Frankfurt–Worms
line'), 849–50 ('I jot down [. . .] too much'), 867 ('My life is useless [. . .] Here
ends my notebook') – with one further quotation from *Hamlet*, I, v, 166–80
('There are more things [. . .] help you, swear').

Eros and Priapus – From fury to ashes. With one more interpolation from
Hamlet, closing monologue of Act II, ii, 551–8, 583–8 ('Is it not [a bit] [. . .]
For Hecuba!'; 'this is most brave [. . .] scullion!'), this section and the next one,
Finale, are again made up entirely of Gadda material – including the words at
the very end, here in small caps – from *Eros e Priapo* (Gadda 1967, EP SGF II
213–374, but see also *Resources* and Italia and Pinotti (2008) for reference to
the forthcoming new Adelphi edition). See SGF II 250 ('It is obvious that [. . .]
desire at bay'), 251–2 ('The furious [. . .] that of the men fowk'), 265 ('And
so. That which [. . .] Motherhood and Infancy'), 265–6 ('Wedding premiums
[. . .] lictor for eternity'), 258 ('And the lack of critical [. . .] critical disquisition'), 266–7 ('It is therefore [. . .] tell you so'), 271 ('But what did he want
[. . .] chopping things off'), 247–8 ('But whoever is in charge [. . .] about in the
muck'), 272 ('He did not know [. . .] false glory'), 222–3 ('Well, the crimes [. . .]
horrendous wreckage'), 225 ('I would like [. . .] do what I can'), 238 ('The collective ego [. . .] or rational knowledge'), 279 ('From a theatrical point of view
[. . .] *they desire him*'), 238–9 ('This does not happen [. . .] bestial revelry'),
227 ('Now this one here [. . .] he finally came'), 230 ('I'm not a psychiatrist'),
231 ('But if someone [. . .] well, here goes'), 342 ('Anyone who appears [. . .]
sometimes of himself'), 343 ('The crazy narcissist [. . .] hanged by the neck'),
345 ('The second aberrant trait [. . .] lack of idolatry'), 347 ('Another mode
[. . .] dung of the world'), 355–6 ('The *content* [. . .] onyx bidet'), 356–7 ('He
shows off [. . .] ovary of the people'), 357 ('The narcissistic manic [. . .] into the
papers'), 348 ('But the dominant trait [. . .] Mr "Ego"'), ibid. ('The lie bursts out
[. . .] can stop it'), 348–9 ('We see the same [. . .] imprisoned for decades'), 356
('ON THE STAGE [. . .] NOTHING ELSE').

Global glossary

Alberto Godioli and Federica G. Pedriali

DEFEAT

Gadda variously iterates the notion of failure. *Giornale* and *Eros e Priapo* centre on glaring DEFEAT and spectacular ruin, two world wars and fascism. Yet DEFEAT predates HISTORY, coinciding with the SUB-JECT's foundational act, *ab ovo* quite literally. Born to be the neglected son. Worse, to be the defective one, out of two sons. The military debacle in this case simply sealed an active paradigm, while the resulting life-long Caporetto forced the further note-taking, the additional accounting, the perfecting of one's failure. The issue is not simply: *why me?* – rather: *what connects people to their fate?* All stories, for Gadda, are about the universe that matters, and the MATTER that finally gets written starts here. Misfortune materialises from either actual guilt, the principle of law or sheer destiny, the principle of tragedy. The former gets correctly and rightfully atoned, but the latter parcels out expiation without reason or explanation. In Gadda's account, some outrages of fortune point to systemic responsibility – ITALY's historical Caporetto. Others just don't, or can't – his personal, his persistent DEFEAT. To say that one pays for somebody else's mistakes may be a good enough comfort trick. Avoiding toughness, however, is not our hero's style. He must tell his story. He won't stop asking Job's question, even though God is bound to be resilient in his answer.

DUCE

The one who leads (*ducere*). The man of destiny. The spirit of HISTORY embodied as superior flesh and bones. This is why great men have got great vision (romantic take). But this is also why they must be up to the task (Gadda's default philosophy as a 'romantic kicked in the pants' –

'Un'opinione sul neorealismo', 1951, VM SGF I 629). A great man's best input must be above all technical. Not by chance, the hero of our hero is the forever watchful and technical Julius Caesar, not that cocky hothead of Bonaparte. Yet, despite having clear parameters, Gadda could be taken in. Mussolini got his public praise, albeit for technical reasons, and he was praised in return for writing technically about the technicalities of the regime. A bit circular, all in all, but highly instructive – especially considering that expiation this time took the form of verbal *retaliation* against the body and name of the DUCE. Of course, for the compromised soldier this was *contrappasso* alright. The more he abused and insulted the ex-leader, the more, in fact, shamed and named he too was – another personal DEFEAT. And here they are, those abusive sweet little nothings (selected them in *M*, in homage, and left untranslated, for there is a limit to what one can ask of translators): *Maccherone fottuto di Predappio, Maldito, Maramaldo, Mascella d'asino Maltone, Merda, Merdone, Minchiolini, Minchione Ottimo Massimo, Modellone Torsolone, Mugliante*. Next letter, first item: *Napoleone fesso e tuttoculo*. For the full listing, some one hundred items, see BI 176–7.

EROS

Evil is EROS in the wrong place. Under fascism, politics in particular turned into a carnival of latent, morbid sexuality. But is there ever the right place for this blind and cruel law? EROS invariably chooses, favouring some, neglecting others. Surely, it never picks the SUBJECT, whose role is, then, that of the excluded party, of the melancholic voyeur. To add insult, as it were, to his injury, exclusion cuts him out for his job. He will be the narrator of EROS' success story. No life of his own, just desire. Potent and even omnipotent in his frustration: but only when paper is the MATTER. A real writer, not just a soldier, and not even just a loser – not someone who stops loving life to bits simply because it does not love you.

HISTORY

There must be a fault somewhere if, as happens in Denmark, time gets out of joint. Inevitably, being entirely spatial and not just pivotal around points of greater stress, time gets differentiated into regions. These may look like nations but are sheer geology, MATTER surfacing from the deep logistics of the planet. We, in turn, are but topsoil – our superior event, that is, is just nature ('Un romanzo giallo nella geologia', 1934

– MdI SGF I 145–51). But can our anthropology really rest there? We must have motion and progress. We must, above all, have HISTORY and cast our hopes before the end sets in. Progress, being concerted action, requires collective persuasion. All sensorial access is legitimate, the aural kind especially, given what the latest reproductive technologies, the sexuality *plus* of the radio and other emerging mass media, expect of the subjects of the leader-DUCE. Forget about death. HISTORY pulls. The future calls. A drilled plurality will get where it populates a lasting belief. The generous mouthwash, going around all mouths, spins the all too renewable yarn. The ball of the world is safe: we are indeed getting back, as fortified belief, the despair we extracted from ourselves and our *sons* (there are no *children*, really, when it comes to the serious MATTER of the continuity of the species). Try to say differently – try, this is but an innocent test. Try to argue that our becoming is nowhere to be seen. That the region is stagnant, that the local lore is a fraud: that this blanket penetration is a crime and that the mafia perpetrating such an inelegant thing is a sad one: a sad oneness of biological intent passing for our getting *there*. Try – if you'd rather disguise your region, given that you are trying in earnest, try ITALY.

ITALY

It is absurd and amazing in one. Italians are resilient in their acqui-escence. You can address them across time and space ('Now, all you Italians of all times and all places [. . .]'). You will always hit upon the stuff of the country, even before the nation, given that there is a geography – 'ITALY is but a geographical definition'. The sentence fuelled the Risorgimento but had its point. The trench doesn't work; a line in ITALY is not a line, especially not a line of people. Or rather, the whole line of the collective effort gets turned into one *shithole* and *hellhole* (the English translation has its advantages over Gadda's original *cesso* and *inferno*); it becomes an anthropology filled with MATTER, and hence also with genius, passion and hard work, all things naturally emerging from the MATTER of life. Even the commitment to the project – reforming the country, make it a nation at last – arises from ITALY's well fertilised anti-linear topsoil. Why, otherwise, go for the desperate measure? The lines of the future, the youth tidied up for the photoshoots of the col-lective aspiration, after so much shithole and hellhole, do give the sense of a large bunch of humans – *fascio*, to the letter – cast adrift in their motherland: at a loss as to the line to take in the international contest of clans. Lombardy thrives on its ninety-degree angles. Our SUBJECT loves the slow advancing line of the bent backs of women working (singing and working) in the nation's tough rice fields ('Dalle mondine, in risaia', 1936, MdI SGF I 175–80, or EP SGF II 268). The local topsoil (what chemical does it lack? what hormone does it overproduce?) imposes that he too joins, officially. And he does – at his earliest convenience.

MATTER

Some of it is called spirit and as such should triumph over the rest. WAR is the clearest test of strength of this order of things. Nothing in fact moves, yet bodies rot and the spirit is knee deep in crap – this on a good day, and when the going gets lucky. If HISTORY is the nightmare (Stephen Dedalus), then the body is HISTORY. But the reality is that MATTER has got too little *vis*, too little of the beckoning of the future to be anything like what we seek through the idea of there being HISTORY. Too little of the hope we stubbornly try to cast past both bog and flow. God knows what else there is out there, in our biochemistry, that could care to know whether we matter at all. When mourning its dead, the body of the soldier notes the inability of the survivors to state what motion exactly has taken place – 'Enrico has gone here, there . . .' Pursuing in image those who are MATTER no more is all the space-time that the SUBJECT will ever be able to synthesise.

NARCISSISM

Or *egotism* – Stendhal introduces the latter term. It is the driving force of nineteenth-century fiction. The hero's (large-minded) self-esteem clashes with (small-minded) society, and the realist novel, the *Bildungsroman* especially, is there to take notes. It is known as the *romantic lie* (Girard 1966) but for Gadda it is as basic as it gets. It is, in one, the key device of communal life: a typically male (de)vice at source (in his reading, women can at worst be vain, not narcissistic), as well as the primary cause of social decay ('The Egoist', 1954 – VM, SGF I 654–66). The social ego in need of praise; the egotic ego of a people overgrown into the ego-cock of the nation; the nation, yes, parading the leader-DUCE as the collectively-wed phallus. All this horror may indeed originate from the even more basic needs of the viscera and primeval hunger (the original *egoism*); yet the resulting modern life, in contemporary universal ITALY, is not just a dull and dangerous myth. Loveless parents, obtuse generals and fanatic tyrants – bless them – have no doubt damaged this one chance, the SUBJECT's only lifetime. However, the real issue is the bloated and mindless nation, the *gens* stranded in sheer NUMBERS and EROS through the lawlessness of that branch of unreason which manifests itself as power and the powerful. Gadda is harsh, brutal, even delirious when it comes to NARCISSISM, and quite rightly so, given what he witnessed. He is the bitter, resentful, vitriolic satirist on such pervasive matters, all the more so because he is also (he denounces it vigorously) the pervaded defective product of a vicious age. His defect, tragically, is simply not defective enough. It doesn't protect from the blessed times. This is why – and it is worth noting in our own diligence – in his attack, as in everything else, he too exhibits the agonistic-egotic cohesion of himself as SUBJECT.

NUMBERS

EROS and nations, having wanted NUMBERS, big NUMBERS, won't provide what NUMBERS require. Forget about boots, those are the luxuries: you are here to work for the mistake. Your host is an exagitated Italian cosmos, 'the universe in specie Italiae' (RI SVP 395). No wonder in this Italian here and now there must be excess (of everything), starting right from the number two (again of everything) – the original excess that saved the day. Only a tough idealism, only an imperative management system based on sheer impersonal procedures can ever hope to stay on top of such conflicting plurality. WAR is absolutely fine, in this respect, and even just, provided it doesn't undo the sums of the nation, what counts as its united NUMBERS. Utopias of totality, the total insanity of Plato, More and Campanella are the mad lesson here. The spell cast by NUMBERS, the awesome aura of the mechanical, the statistical and the quantifiable, the amazing sex appeal of mathematics and geometry, the exciting frigidity of the abstract, the formal and the analytical – all this, in sum (oh yes, you see, *in sum*), calculates the command, delivers the purely numerical regime that will set ITALY right and on its course. Our reject too – our SUBJECT – odd and single as he is, cannot resist the industrial charm of big NUMBERS. As a scientist, he definitely loves the perpetuation of the species he was determined to miss as a man. He loves also, but this is a minor numerical foible, his most personal identification number, his date of birth. Hence, and systematically, fourteen of everything – as in dates of things done or to do. As if somewhere in NUMBERS there could be reproductive luck for him too.

SHAKESPEARE

Time is out of joint and Denmark is a prison. For the anti-hero the only action left under these conditions may look like inaction but is a positive negative, resistance actively arising from life as shadow and seasonless exclusion. 'Hamlet's mission is, inevitably, a *negative* one' ('*Amleto* al Teatro Valle', 1952 – VM, SGF I 540). Life is a tale told by an idiot – or better still: 'What we call HISTORY should rather be defined as a farce acted by natural born idiots' ('L'Editore chiede venia del recupero', 1963 – CdD, RR I 761). This is a farce that indeed never forgets that tragedy thrives on impurity of means: 'The advertisement of the San Remo Casino, published while another grenadier was dying slaughtered in Doberdò, is a masterpiece of decay and mockery. But it is a master-piece, a page worthy of SHAKESPEARE' ('The second book of Poetics', 1928 – Qdi, 2, 2003: 20). Gonzalo even has his Hamletic monologue ('What is nobler? To seize the lying kiss of Appearance [. . .] Or rather to plunge her into rancour and contempt?' – CdD RR I 703 at source), although like Hamlet, he is beyond his dilemma, his procedural doubt regarding the guilty party having been neatly sorted out a long time ago ('*Amleto*' – VM SGF I 540). In a Shakespearean nutshell: *fair is foul, foul is fair*. Life, that is, fully deserves the authorial cauldron, the magic of creative retribution, the exposure of its hard core of filth through the stripping action of this high-temperature WRITING. The naked life extracted in this way of course is still literature: full-bodied, saturating and rich in artifice (technically *devices*). Desperate as the hope of cure may sound, the essence of an antidote of sorts, the only one possible perhaps, nonetheless works its minimal wonder, releasing the belief that in this literature, in this *unpacking of one's heart with words* ('And fall a-cursing, like a very drab, a scullion!') may be found 'the unavoidable tool for the discovery and the enunciation of truth' ('*Amleto*' – VM SGF I 541). Not by chance, Gadda's hope continues to revolve around *Hamlet*, right from '*Amleto* al Teatro Valle' – far more than a theatre review, nothing less than a personal manifesto.

SUBJECT

'I am going mad. I should go up to Pirandello and ask him to make me a character in his plays' (Gadda 1984: 106). The SUBJECT may be a degenerative fiction but has got a role to play. He must step in and take the initiative where there is no such thing or chance. The nation, the *gens* has forsaken the call – HISTORY, the future. And even though our hero is weak, he can turn that weakness into the energy supply that will see him through his demolition task, on behalf of us all somehow, despite there also being exclusivity in his claims. Yes, Gadda is full of identity, for a purpose, even though he has missed the purpose of his life. Or perhaps not, let's not indulge in that myth, however tempting. Like the DUCE, our SUBJECT is a straightforward technical issue, his name and his arguments those of a 'nobody without the right preparation for life' (Gadda 1984: 76). Not by chance, on his capture the enemy did not bother to shoot; you don't simply waste good ammunition on MATTER already disinvested by life. And yet, although his martyrdom (no other technical term will do) must be of no interest to anyone, this *no one* that hasn't got the learning, the strength, the time or the paper to work out the argument proving the error of the world (resources are scarce all round, especially the supporting agency of destiny or God, which his gesture nonetheless requires) has earned for himself the ultimate technical mission, the finally *legitimate* task.

THEATRE

All the world's a stage – everyone to one's part, out of hypocrisy or necessity. It takes immense willpower to step aside and transcend it all as in a Quevedo masterpiece of baroque satire. Gadda knew well (and translated) *The World as It Is* (*Il mondo com'è*, 1941, SVP 265–95). In Gifuni's play, in addition, he gets to know an exception and a compensation by taking literally centre stage, the proxemics usually claimed by egotists and tyrants. Aware as he is of the provocation of his oneness, through Gifuni, through THEATRE more generally, Gadda comes to the limelight of his singularity – contrary to his photophobic plea ('Please, leave me in the shadow' – Gadda 1993: 186). Contrary, that is, to his habitual role as the serviceable author turned petulant narrator and lending Life the non-life she needs to prove that she can indeed command misery. A shadowy population of such alter egos inhabits this fiction, among the sudden, bitter-lyrical movements of the satirical-forlorn original observer. Yet, strictly speaking, none of this is THEATRE, even though all of it shouts its theatrical quality, language gone onstage for all to hear, and displaying its own histrionic risk. Few other writers in the entire Italian canon get to know, as successfully, this exception and this compensation: the aural feel of their own words on stage. Few lend themselves to be read aloud, vocalised and performed as brilliantly as Gadda. It is no chance, it cannot be, that the line of actors and directors busying themselves with this NON-THEATRE is getting exceptionally long and varied – from the splendidly produced Luca Ronconi (*Quer pastic-ciaccio*, 1996) to Fabrizio Gifuni's daring stark centre stage (*L'ingegner Gadda va alla guerra*, here and now).

VOICE

The world as error explained. If we are to become collectively plural (genuinely plural: schizophrenic pluralism won't do – Nancy 2000), there must be collaboration across divides. The masses, on the one hand, must accept their status and state, and be pliable, inert, female, ready to be impressed, to be given shape – more classically still, to be given *form*. The heuristic principle, on the other hand, must play the shape-giver and father, his mission being equally one of transcendence and sacrifice. MATTER, the *res extensa*, is pulled, in fact, to extend beyond extension itself: brave new synthetic worlds must be delivered through the colonial conquest of the unnatural globe of the mind. The cue may come from the contemporary local wars, yet the idea is truly timeless – and the masses will always be there and willing, for unless you really provoke them or starve them, they will do as told. The telling is also exceedingly straightforward: almost anything that gets uttered will be repeated and passed round. Nowadays, it even gets recorded, amplified and broad-cast, as if previous control technologies, oral culture and officialdom – the state, science and religion – had not been thorough, not inhumane enough. The process – the mistake, the erring world – gets then finalised – completed and sealed – through the seminal speech of the leader-DUCE (*il Verbo*). Like indeed the Liquid (yes, that liquid), such conclusive action exploits gravity to come down on the masses, to bless them with reproduction. *Sgrondare* (the word runs riot in the rioting *Eros e Priapo*) from the height of the speech balcony in Piazza Venezia is exactly what Derrida, in another theoretical scenario, cannot but call, quite literally, *dissemination*. It may be a bit of a blanket method, but reproduction seldom fails. It is a real pity, of course, that nature is not organised more sensitively; pity, above all, that its selections of the fittest invariably choose the laziest speech. And yet the young are so cute, so convinc-ing, in their praise of their dear father. Only a very few, only Adorno (*Minima moralia*), only Gadda (*Eros e Priapo*), are dismayed by that tiny VOICE, by that little hysterical chant of the young gathered in educa-tion and thanksgiving. 'In fascism, the nightmare of childhood realised itself' (*Minima moralia*, § 123). Only the singular THEATRE, with its own peculiar vocal counter-projection, as Pirandello would see it, can withstand the radio and the gramophone of the age, the emission of *His*

Master's Voice (here both brand name and reference to the Maker, that brute gravitational force which in the time of the new mass media even goes on air, gets airborne).

WAR

Misquoting the Bard again – *all is fair in love and war*. Or ultra-Shakespeareanly: *all is foul in love and war*. Be it foul or fair, polemos – as much as EROS – is the law. *Bellum omnium contra omnes* (Hobbes). *Struggle for life* (Darwin). Lose or win it (appear to), everyone goes to WAR, with no clear reasons or explanations for either outcomes. Transcending the ego, sacrificing oneself in the name of a higher stance – mostly the homeland – may be one of the added local objectives. It is in this sense that Gadda 'sought and loved military life' (CdU, RR I 142; Roscioni 1997: 124–5), going to the WAR available to him with enthusiasm, his own annihilation-sublimation being among his highest hopes. Needless to say, such love was unrequited. Polemos left the soldier to the gloomy dungeon of his insufficient body and inertial destiny (*going nowhere*, after Caporetto), while his local HISTORY continued to rage past the official end of the hostilities. But *war is the father of all things* (Heraclitus). The local logistics, including the fake warring unities of homeland and SUBJECT, are bound to fail – they are meant to. Gadda acknowledges this, through his understanding of early twentieth century physics and psychoanalysis. Whether in here, in our HISTORY, or out there, the universe is just an ever-changing system of colliding forces possessing all, driving nations and individuals alike: making them passing instantiations of the assertive vigour (*vis*) which keeps going to nature's WAR – *à l'amour comme à la guerre*.

WRITING

Isn't he too, the WRITING SUBJECT, exactly like the DUCE, a champion of prompt mimesis? With the help of a reactive liver, his senses – sight, smell, hearing especially – have synthesised the times, as well as time, and can now regurgitate the ultimate default perversion: the spirit of the age ('each generation to its own wisdom' – L'A, RR I 557). However, unlike one's own age, especially unlike *him*, who 'did not know the anguish', the negated SUBJECT has *known*, and his negatives are invariably technical ('No one knew the slow pallor of denial', CdD RR I 703; *Acquainted with Grief*, 1969: 155). Having nowhere else to turn to now, this counter-egotistic histrionic ham goes, in fact, to his further WAR. He is the giant of negation saturating the available page-stage in return for the evil shared. It looks like a mad gamble: he can stun us with his tongue: he can speak in tongues. Yet his amazing technical feat is also sold to the devil that he is. Through it – reader, beware – your writer is claiming his share of absolute leadership, like the infernal *portitor* itself (EP SGF II 219), like time that is. You will go, just watch it, through the retribution he offers, sensing that the promise of resurrection is not generous and depends entirely on the SUBJECT's terms. This is why, again technically – *techne* is the one thing worth holding on to – he cannot, he will not be *everyone* or *everyman*. Only the imploded singular self, in its awareness, can exert its pull, taking the place of the only available future, of the one chance of positive HISTORY we missed. It imposes, you have no alternative, the re-direction of the horrific flow: everything and everyone must pass through *his* final judgment. This confirms, of course, the various theories regarding the dangers of the hypertrophic SUBJECT in respect of the usefulness of the containing collective. However, to be the most counter-invasive entry remains a duty – there is really no arguing with this, given life's GLOSSARY. And have you noticed? This is also how our rough guide to our SUBJECT reaches its *explicit* on the fourteenth item.

APPENDIX

Gadda, Heal Thyself

Federica G. Pedriali

The senses under fascism? They did their job, they were but conduits – the new mandatory standards had to be poured into the person. They were, yes, the chamber pots of the Reform, of the superposition of the State over the individual and the nation. Oh, what goodness, what justice, what nobility of the plan and the planner! But also what non-sense, what absolute ridiculousness, what horror at the time and ever since, because humanity is incorrigible, and Plato incurable: because Our Boss and Great Mind only led us to the spectacle of our infinite shame.

Something, that is, in the general corruption, given the pressure of the collective, ended up resisting. Was this the myth of a personal, of a *sensory* antifascism? Gadda disassociated himself *straightaway* from the *associates* – this is the resisting myth of *Eros e Priapo*. In the overall desperation of the senses, he could boast, in fact, a fine nose. A knowing nose. Like San Carlo Borromeo's, like a breakwater, to cut through destiny. And moreover a sinus – truly a pipe – capacious, powerful, sensitive. Without hesitation, it had classified fascism as the stench of dying matter. Was is enough, to be absolved, having that eroticised nose of the age? Could it be enough to have grunted and wallowed in the unreason of the times, in order to denounce it? Those of ill will, who by caste privilege understand these matters, have another opinion. He held his nose, they say: he held it tight.

But myths, inevitably, must gloss over certain details. Gadda did defend the Reform to the last, was one of the last to stop defending it, this being one of those details – with the Duce, *il Merda* as he was too soon indeed to call him in the role, of course, of Grand Reformer. Just technical articles, no doubt: perhaps of no political import, but hey. And in any case, the articles shaped, could undoubtedly shape opinion, if there was still any need to do so. Quite possibly, in actual fact, there was more need than ever, seeing how times had turned, starting with his own very need, the need of the Dissociated One, of the one increasingly excluded party, with his dissociable senses: the excluded one, that is, from the *happy*, from the *free* and *fair* circulation of the Hopes of the Nation. He had been a soldier. He had not known demobilisation from the Roman ideal of the *patria*, of the *gens*. Those who say that, as a good soldier, he held his post above and beyond the call of his duty are, in fact, quite correct.

The new mandatory standard, and an individual outwith every standard, and still a creature born of the Standard. The sickness of the senses was almost a schizophrenia, or more precisely, a schizophrenic echolalia, because this was how the ear was used. It was a chamber pot, and the person, a bunged up sinus-pipe, couldn't but blow out horrendous collective liquids. Perhaps for this reason, a clear distinction between fascism and antifascism, in Gadda, cannot be fished from the filthy water. On this topic our writer is most definitely contradictory, mendacious: too compromised on both sides of the coin, in his mocking Leibnizian way. Two incompossible values coexist, in his case, on the same coin, a merging of faith and the absurdity of faith that is not for gain or logic – even though actually, logically, here we should talk of logical coexistence, and in the sense that Gadda liked best. The somewhat partisan congeniality of the epistemic positions taken in *Meditazione milanese* stand witness. The impasse, in fact and in practice, was not solved with the solutions of history – how could it be?

Winter 1944–5: Gadda is evacuated from Florence. This is the guy who turns his hand to *Eros e Priapo*, who does not resist images of the liberating *fianta*, the ferrying of mobs, the infernal signposts of the future. From *here*, through *this* death, through *this* text, the way of *resurrection* as the total consciousness of the nation to be retried implicitly – after an eternity of condemnation. To be retried, indeed, with different or rather, with less foolish and credulous, sure, but still total and totalising sublimation, in the actual transfer from *this* madness to a future *reasonableness*. It is not by chance that, like a good ferryman, Gadda left in the Order of the Implicits, alas!, the confession that applied to him: the mention of the long Chapter of Civil Hope under fascism, his support for the regime. Perhaps he really did ferry dishonestly. Perhaps he could not have strategised better, who knows. As if to say: strategising for the right ends.

It is always legitimate to distinguish the narrator from the copywriter. If a technical distinction can save the technical Gadda, autarchic ambassador, that's good, and in a way justice is done, from one service provider to another service provider, from human being to human being. Here, however, before taking our leave from our translational provocations, we must consider something else and something other, if we are to make sense of the debate surrounding this Gadda; we must dare look back, conclusively, into the schizophrenic unity of experience, where the real horror is that of the cohesion of the most absurd coexistence. Wasn't Gadda the first to say that he felt himself to be responsible? For his present position, yes, just as he was for his own written thoughts? In his thought and written present – this is the indistinguishable fact – a particular, an aggravated sense of fullness: like a brimming cemetery well, among promiscuous effusions of internal fluids, no possibilities excluded, not even that which would camouflage Eros as penitent Eros, so as to relaunch the forever absent and ineffable Logos. A complicated endocrine profile, perhaps. Certainly, the collapse of the one and only army-issue moral consciousness.

Opposites arise by contiguity. From the *patria*, from the myth of the high *polis*, the low antipode: the subject's take on the upside-down world. From his *Meraviglie d'Italia*, his *Cognizione*. From this, the drift towards *Adalgisa*. In that, in a book declaredly destined for times of peace (a paradoxical destination: what times are ever peaceful?), the further general rehearsal of the *flumen inferi*, the other tragic-comic mouthwash of an entire culture: the other major restitution – before the *Mess* – of the poison received, and with interest. The regulatory plan. Humanity as a disastrous Milanese sewer system. The full fruit of this maturity was a *stagione splendida* for those with a nose for such things. The first two great novels, the promise of the third. One forkful after another in the phenomenal, while we are waiting for the divine garden fork. The horrific subterranean declination of the phrasal standards, his own and of his time, on the reverse of the celebration of the fascist reordering of the Drains. Gadda's long Sabbath was, in truth, an endless thing.

Those happy few who refer this death to that other splendid moment of suffering – the preceding season of the *Meditazione* – are quite right to do so. The territorial, the colonial advancement of reason, or rather, its conquest of the political space; the glorious sacrifice of the individual in a greater, vaster meaning; its total functionalisation in the name of the Project. Which does not mean to say – careful now – that in his much-praised expansive and expansionist $n + 1$ we are or would be less restricted, less oppressed. That pleistocene processor of the brain, which computes with a genuine euphoria, for its good and ours, what our duty will be in the progress of the Mind, offers totality, complexity, mythical numbers as incentive and in compensation for the sacrifice. But should we trust it? Every utopia, it is quite true, assigns its own rigid merchandise – so much goes to the individual, so much to the collective – quantifying the unverifiables of a conviviality which is imagined, one does really try, in the most civilised manner possible. But *Meditazione* is no utopia, even if it originates, like much philosophy, from a peculiar despair regarding the social. In fact, aren't its incentives those of an innocently Milanese epistemology, of an *apolitical* order of reflection? Of an order, that is, that has nothing to do with *that* project of simplification, the fascist Reform of Italian-ness? It is like that for most readers: *Meditazione* and fascism? Nonsense. Gadda's fascism? Or was it anti-fascism? Without question or doubt, the time that was splendid was indeed some time, *woe unto you, ye souls of the depraved* – while the remainders of the day were entirely taken up, again, by the Standards of Time.

Translated by Christopher John Ferguson

Endnote

To be strictly Gaddian about things, *Our Boss and Great Mind* is not an epithet of Gadda's making, no need to check the Indices in the Garzanti edition under the much-named *Mussolini Benito* (BI 176–7). The title of this Appendix is instead adapted from Gadda's own exclamative 'O Plato, cùrati!' (EP SGF II 234). Many are the borrowings, especially from *Eros e Priapo*. A list wouldn't keep trace of all the debts, but here is one anyway, minimally reasoned out: EP SGF II 219–20 (*portitor*, ferryman: with Dantean and Virgilian echoes), 221 (*associati*, associates: the word on which *Eros e Priapo* gets going, with the idea soon doubled by the *dissociation*, from the associates, and in a psychological sense), 230–1 (*naso*, nose: first mention of the item, and immediately a central concept, in this work as elsewhere), 232 (*transitus*, transfer: from madness to reasonableness – one of the many signs of the resilience of belief), 243 (mouthwash: the most cited occurrence is in the 1949 essay 'Come lavoro', VM SGF I 436), 251 (echolalia: one of the keywords of *Eros e Priapo*; also circulating widely, among other texts, in the 1958 essay collection *I viaggi la morte*), 273 (dying matter: the Gaddian theme par excellence – much varied, here and in our *Global glossary*, as well as in the chapter *Staging*), 285 (*fianta liberatrice*, of the liberators: one of the various instances, in *Eros e Priapo*, and combining Liberation, Nemesis and scatological considerations), 316 (chamber pot of the senses: with the ear as the item itself), 328 (other side of the coin: literally), 346 (complicated endocrine portrait: well established theme with good samples in the earlier *Meditazione*, which also gave the pleistocene brain-processor, MM SVP 666, 714 – an alternative could have been the brain-uterus, SVP 721, but this somehow made getting to utopias and their accountancy less straightforward); 350 (cemetery well: the outcome, the end, yes the place where every list must stop). *Woe unto you* comes from Dante, *Inf.*, III, 84. Among the Gaddian mannerisms that it has given the most pleasure to adopt are: *oh!* (L'A RR I 306–8, introducing the sewer motif of the novel destined for *normal*, for *peaceful* times, cf. RR I 839), *ahi!* (EP SGF II 231).

Bibliography

Primary bibliography

Unless otherwise indicated, Gadda's works are referenced using the five-volume edition, plus Indices, of the *Opere*, edited by Dante Isella (Milan: Garzanti, 1988–93) and abbreviated as RR I, RR II, SGF I, SGF II, SVP and BI (see *Abbreviations*). Titles are given in English only where an English translation exists and reference is being made to it. Unless referenced to an existing English translation, primary quotations in English are in-house translations.

Other editions/works cited

(1984) *L'ingegner fantasia. Lettere a Ugo Betti. 1919–1930*, edited by G. Ungarelli, Milan: Rizzoli.
(1987) *La cognizione del dolore*, critical edition by E. Manzotti, Turin: Einaudi.
(1993) *'Per favore mi lasci nell'ombra'. Interviste 1950–1972*, edited by C. Vela, Milan: Adelphi Edizioni.
(2011) *Accoppiamenti giudiziosi (1924–1958)*, edited by P. Italia and G. Pinotti, Milan: Adelphi Edizioni.

Volume titles (with main volume editions and standard abbreviations)

A   *Gli Anni*, Florence: Parenti, 1943; Turin: Einaudi, 1964².
AG   *Accoppiamenti giudiziosi (I Racconti – 1924–1958)*, Milan: Garzanti, 1963.
Az   *Azoto e altri scritti di divulgazione scientifica*, edited by V. Scheiwiller and presented by A. Silvestri, Milan: Libri Scheiwiller, 1986.
BC   *Le bizze del capitano in congedo e altri racconti*, Milan: All'insegna del pesce d'oro, 1981; Adelphi Edizioni, 1981, 1983².
CdD   *La cognizione del dolore*, Turin: Einaudi, 1963; with two additional chapters, 1970⁴.

CdU   *Il castello di Udine*, Florence: Edizioni di Solaria, 1934; Turin: Einaudi, 1955².

EP   *Eros e Priapo (da furore a cenere)*, Milan: Garzanti, 1967.

F220   *Un fulmine sul 220*, Milan: Garzanti, 2000.

GASP   *Il guerriero, l'amazzone, lo spirito della poesia nel verso immortale del Foscolo – Conversazione a tre voci*, Milan: Garzanti, 1967.

GB   *Gonnella buffone*, Parma: Guanda, 1985.

GGP   *Giornale di guerra e di prigionia*, Florence: Sansoni, 1955; Turin: Einaudi, 1965².

L'A   *L'Adalgisa – Disegni milanesi*, Florence: Le Monnier, 1944, 1945²; Turin: Einaudi, 1955³.

LdF   *I Luigi di Francia*, Milan: Garzanti, 1964.

M   *La meccanica*, Milan: Garzanti, 1970.

MdF   *La Madonna dei Filosofi*, Florence: Edizioni di Solaria, 1931; Turin: Einaudi, 1955².

MdI   *Le meraviglie d'Italia*, Florence: Parenti, 1939; Turin: Einaudi, 1964².

MdS   *I miti del somaro*, edited by A. Andreini, Milan: Libri Scheiwiller, 1988.

MM   *Meditazione milanese*, Turin: Einaudi, 1974.

NdF   *Novelle dal Ducato in fiamme*, Florence: Vallecchi, 1953.

NS   *Novella seconda*, Milan: Garzanti, 1971.

PLF   *Il primo libro delle Favole*, Venice: Pozza, 1952.

PdO   *Il palazzo degli ori*, Turin: Einaudi, 1983.

QP   *Quer pasticciaccio brutto de via Merulana*, Milan: Garzanti, 1957.

RI   *Racconto italiano di ignoto del novecento (Cahier d'études)*, Turin: Einaudi, 1983.

SF   *I sogni e la folgore*, Turin: Einaudi, 1955.

SS   *Un radiogramma per modo di dire e scritti sullo spettacolo*, Milan: Il Saggiatore, 1982.

Te   *Il Tevere*, edited by D. Isella, Lugano, Milan and New York: Annuario della Fondazione Schlesinger, 1991.

TO   *Il tempo e le opere – Saggi, note e divagazioni*, Milan: Adelphi Edizioni, 1982.

VlC   *Verso la Certosa*, Milan and Naples: Ricciardi, 1961.

VM   *I viaggi la morte*, Milan: Garzanti, 1958.

VS   *La verità sospetta – Tre traduzioni di C. E. Gadda*, Milan: Bompiani, 1977.

English translations

La cognizione del dolore
(1969)   *Acquainted with Grief*, trans. by W. Weaver, New York: Braziller and London: Owen. Then (1985) New York: Braziller. Chapters 3 and 5 also in *EJGS* BabelGadda.

La Madonna dei Filosofi
(2008)   *The Philosophers' Madonna*, trans. by A. Melville, London: Atlas.

L'incendio di via Keplero
(1964)   'The fire on Via Keplero', trans. by W. Weaver, *Art and Literature*, 1 (March): 18–30.
(1998)   'The fire on Kepler Street', trans. by A. B. Hartley, *Forum Italicum*, 32, 1: 219–31. Also in *EJGS* BabelGadda.

Quer pasticciaccio brutto de via Merulana
(1965)   *That Awful Mess on Via Merulana*, trans. by W. Weaver, New York: Braziller. Then (1966) London: Secker & Warburg; (1984) with an introduction by I. Calvino, New York: Braziller; (1985) London: Quartet encounters. Extracts from Chapters 1–2, 4–6, 9–10 also in *EJGS* BabelGadda.
(2000)   'A New Annotated Translation of C. E. Gadda's *Quer pasticciaccio brutto de via Merulana*', trans. by R. de Lucca, *Forum Italicum*, 34, 1: 270–86. Also in *EJGS* BabelGadda.

French translations

Accoppiamenti giudiziosi
(1989)   *Des accouplements bien réglés*, trans. by F. Dupuigrenet Desroussilles and M. Fratnik, Paris: Seuil.

Eros e Priapo (Da furore a cenere)
(1990)   *Eros et Priape – De la fureur aux cendres*, trans. by G. Clerico, Paris: Bourgois.

Fuga a Tor di Nona
(1987)   *Fuite à Tor di Nona*, trans. by J.-P. Manganaro, *EJGS* BabelGadda.

Giornale di guerra e di prigionia
(1993)   *Journal de guerre et de captivité*, preface by M. Baccelli and G.-G. Lémaire, trans. by M. Baccelli, Paris: Bourgois.

Gli anni; Verso la Certosa
(2002)   *Les années; Vers la Chartreuse*, preface by G. G. Lémaire, trans. and commentary by J.-P. Manganaro, Paris: Bourgois.

Il castello di Udine
[1982] (1991)   *Le Château d'Udine*, introduction by M. Fusco, trans. by G. Clerico, Paris: Grasset.

Il guerriero, l'amazzone, lo spirito della poesia nel verso immortale del Foscolo – Conversazione a tre voci
(1993)   *Le guerrier, l'amazone, l'esprit de la poésie dans le vers immortel de Foscolo (Conversation à trois voix)*, trans. by J.-P. Manganaro, Paris: Bourgois. Also in *EJGS* BabelGadda.

Il palazzo degli ori
(1989)   *Le Palais des ors*, trans. by B. Sayhi-Périgot, Paris: Quai Voltaire.

Il primo libro delle Favole
(2000)   *Le premier livre des fables*, preface by G.-G. Lémaire, trans. by
J. Pastureau, Paris: Bourgois.

Il tempo e le opere – Saggi, note e divagazioni
(1994)   *Le temps et les oeuvres: essais, notes et digressions*, edited by
D. Férault, Paris: Le Promeneur.

I Luigi di Francia
(1989)   *Les Louis de France*, trans. by C. Paoloni, Paris: Quai Voltaire.

I viaggi la morte
(1994)   *Les voyages la mort*, preface by G.-G. Lémaire, trans. by M. Baccelli,
Paris: Bourgois.

La cognizione del dolore
[1983] (1987)   *La Connaissance de la douleur*, trans. by L. Bonalumi and
F. Wahl, Paris: Seuil.

L'Adalgisa – Disegni milanesi
[1987] (1997)   *L'Adalgisa – Croquis milanais*, trans. by J.-P. Manganaro,
Paris: Seuil.

La Madonna dei Filosofi
(1993)   *La Madone des Philosophes. Récits*, trans. by J.-P. Manganaro,
Paris: Seuil.

Lu meccanica
(1992)   *La Mécanique*, preface by D. Isella, trans. by Ph. Di Meo, Paris:
Seuil.

Le bizze del capitano in congedo e altri racconti
(1989)   *Les Colères du capitaine en congé libérable et autres récits*, trans. by
F. Rosso, Paris: Seuil.

Le meraviglie d'Italia
(1998)   *Les Merveilles d'Italie*, preface by G.-G. Lémaire, trans. by
J.-P. Manganaro, Paris: Bourgois.

Lettere a Gianfranco Contini
(1988)   *Lettres à Gianfranco Contini*, afterword by P. Mauriès, trans. by
S. Aghion, Paris: Quai Voltaire.

Norme per la redazione di un testo radiofonico
(1993)   *L'art d'écrire pour la radio*, edited by G. Monsaingeon, Paris: Les
Belles Lettres.

Novella seconda
(1987)   *Novella seconda*, preface by G.-G. Lémaire, trans. by G. Joppolo,
A. Luciani, Th.-O. Séchan, Paris: Bourgois.

Paragrafo della virginità
(1997)   *Paragraphe de la virginité*, trans. by J.-P. Manganaro. Also in *EJGS*
BabelGadda.

Quer pasticciaccio brutto de via Merulana
[1963, 1983] (1999) *L'Affreux Pastis de la rue des Merles*, trans. by
L. Bonalumi, Paris: Seuil.
(2007)   'Tous désormais l'appelaient' (incipit of *Pasticciaccio*, RR II 15–29),
trans. by F. Sicamois. *EJGS* BabelGadda, The French Files, *EJGS*
5/2005.

Racconto italiano di ignoto del novecento
(1997)   *Récit italien d'un inconnu du vingtième siècle*, preface by
G.-G. Lémaire, trans. by M. Baccelli, Paris: Bourgois.

German translations

Accoppiamenti giudiziosi
[1987]   (1992) *Cupido im Hause Brocchi*, trans. by T. Kienlechner, Berlin:
Wagenbach. Then (1995) Frankfurt am Main: Fischer. Contents:
'San Giorgio in casa Brocchi'.
(1988)   *List und Tücke – Erzählungen*, trans. by T. Kienlechner, Berlin:
Wagenbach. Contents: 'Papà e mamma'; 'Accoppiamenti giudiziosi';
'Cugino barbiere'; 'Una buona nutrizione'; 'Dopo il silenzio'; 'Socer
generque'.

A un amico fraterno – Lettere a Bonaventura Tecchi
(1990)   *An einen brüderlichen Freund – Briefe an Bonaventura Tecchi*, trans.
by W. Börner, Frankfurt am Main: Suhrkamp.

Eros e Priapo (da furore a cenere)
(1991)   *Eros und Priapos*, trans. by W. Börner, Frankfurt am Main:
Suhrkamp.

I Luigi di Francia
(1966)   *Frankreichs Ludwige*, trans. by T. Kienlechner, München: Hanser.

La cognizione del dolore
[1964, 1985] (1992) *Die Erkenntnis des Schmerzes*, afterword by
H. M. Enzensberger, trans. by T. Kienlechner, München: Piper. Also
(1974) Frankfurt am Main: Suhrkamp; (2000) Berlin: Wagenbach.

L'Adalgisa – Disegni milanesi
(1989)   *Adalgisa*, trans. by T. Kienlechner, Berlin: Wagenbach. Then (1994)
Frankfurt am Main: Fischer.
(1991)   *Vier Töchter und jede eine Königin. Mailänder Skizzen*, trans. by
T. Kienlechner, Berlin: Wagenbach.

La meccanica
(1992)   *La Meccanica*, trans. by M. Schneider, Frankfurt am Main:

Suhrkamp. Then (1993) as *Der Liebe zur Mechanik*, Frankfurt am Main: Suhrkamp.

Le meraviglie d'Italia – Gli anni
[1985, 1992] (1998) *Die Wunder Italiens*, trans. by T. Kienlechner, Berlin: Wagenbach.

Quer pasticciaccio brutto de via Merulana
(1961) *Die grässliche Bescherung in der Via Merulana*, trans. by T. Kienlechner, München: Piper. Then (1965) Kornwestheim: Europäischer Buchklub; (1966) Frankfurt am Main and Hamburg: Fischer Bücherei; (1974) with afterword by A. Antkowiak, Berlin: Volk und Welt; (1979) Darmstadt: Luchterhand; (1985) Stuttgart and München: Demschen Bücherbundes; (1986, 1988, 1991) München and Zürich: Piper; (1995) Frankfurt am Main: Suhrkamp; (1998) Rheda Wiedenbrück, Wien and Zürich: Bertelsmann.

Collections

(1965)   *Erzählungen*, trans. by H. Riedt, Frankfurt am Main: Suhrkamp.
(1993)   *Mein Mailand. Ein Lese- und Bilderbuch* (based on *La Milano disparsa di C. E. Gadda*, Milan: Garzanti, 1983), trans. by T. Kienlechner, Berlin: Wagenbach.

Spanish and Catalan translations

Accoppiamenti giudiziosi
(1971)   *Acoplamientos juiciosos – Relatos completos 1924/1958*, trans. by E. Guasta, Caracas: Monte Avila Editores.

La cognizione del dolore
(1965)   *Aprendizaje del dolor*, trans. by J. Petit and J. R. Masoliver, Barcelona: Seix Barral. Then (1989) with an introduction by G. Contini, trans. by M. N. Muñiz, Madrid: Ediciones Catedra; (2011) trans. by J. Petit, J. R. Masoliver and M. N. Muñiz, Barcelona: Días contados.
(1992)   *Le coneixença del dolor*, trans. by X. Riu, Barcelona: Edicions 62. Catalan translation.

La meccanica
(1971)   *La Mecánica*, trans. by F. Serra Cantarell, Barcelona: Barral Editores.

Quer pasticciaccio brutto de via Merulana
[1965, 1984] (1990) *El zafarrancho aquel de via Merulana*, trans. by J. R. Masoliver, Barcelona: Seix Barral. Also (1985) Bogotà: Oveja Negra.
(1995)   *Quell merdé hurrible de via Merulana*, trans. by J. Julià, Barcelona: Edicions Proa. Catalan translation.

Collections

(1970) *Dos relatos y un ensayo*, trans. by F. Serra Cantarell, Barcelona: Tusquets.

Cited secondary bibliography

Adamo, Sergia (2004) 'Gadda e Dostoevskij', in Manzotti and Pedriali (2004).

Adorno, Theodor W. [1951] (2006) *Minima Moralia: Reflections from Damaged Life*, London and New York: Verso Books.

Agosti, Stefano (1995) 'Quando il linguaggio non va in vacanza: una lettura del *Pasticciaccio*', in Terzoli (1995: 247–63).

Amigoni, Ferdinando (1995) *La più semplice macchina. Lettura freudiana del 'Pasticciaccio'*, Bologna: il Mulino. Chapter 1 also in *EJGS* Archives.

Andreini, Alba (2004) 'La fortuna del *Pasticciaccio*', in Manzotti and Pedriali (2004).

Andreini, Alba and Tessari, Roberto (eds) (2001) *La letteratura in scena. Gadda e il teatro*, Rome: Bulzoni.

Anglani, Bartolo (2004) 'Le guerre di Gaddus (Da Stendhal a Céline)', in C. Mileschi (ed.), *Dire la guerre?*, Special issue of *Cahiers d'études italiennes*, 1: 39–53.

Antonello, Pierpaolo (2003) 'Opinò Cartesio. Monismo cognitivo e materia pensante in Gadda', *EJGS* Regular Issue, 3, *EJGS* 3/2003.

Antonello, Pierpaolo (2004) 'Gadda e il darwinismo', in Manzotti and Pedriali (2004).

Antonello, Pierpaolo (2005) 'Il mondo come sistema di relazioni: il pasticciaccio gnoseologico dell'ingegnere Carlo Emilio Gadda', in *Il 'ménage' a quattro. Scienza, filosofia, tecnica nella letteratura italiana del Novecento*, Florence: Le Monnier, pp. 22–78.

Appiah, Kwame Anthony (1993) 'Thick translation', *Callaloo*, 16, 4 (Autumn): 808–19.

Arbasino, Alberto (2008) *L'Ingegnere in blu*, Milan: Adelphi Edizioni.

Baldi, Valentino (2010) *Reale invisibile. Mimesi e interiorità nella narrativa di Pirandello e Gadda*, Venice: Marsilio.

Benedetti, Carla (1995) 'La storia naturale nell'opera di Gadda', in M.-H. Caspar (ed.), *Carlo Emilio Gadda, Italies. Narrativa*, 7, Paris: Université Paris X – Nanterre, pp. 71–89; also in *EJGS* Archives.

Benedetti, Carla (2004a) 'Gadda e il pensiero della complessità', in Savettieri et al. (2004: 11–30).

Benedetti, Carla (2004b) 'Carlo Emilio Gadda e la goia del narrare', in P. Amalfitano (ed.), *Le emozioni nel romanzo. Dal comico al patetico*, Rome: Bulzoni, pp. 191–207; also in *EJGS* Archives.

Benedetti, Carla (2011) 'Gadda e l'astrazione narrativa', in Pedriali (2011a).

Benjamin, Walter [1936] (1968) 'The Storyteller', in *Illuminations*, edited by H. Arendt, New York: Schocken Books.

Bernini, Marco (2011) 'Manifestare territori acustici. Il personaggio in Gadda, Bachtin, Deleuze', *EJGS* Regular Issue 7, *EJGS* 7/2011.

Bertone, Manuela (2004) '"Nel magazzino, nel retrobottega del cervello / Within the book and volume of my brain": per l'*Amleto* di Carlo Emilio Gadda', in Savettieri et al. (2004: 105–36).

Bertone, Manuela (ed.) (2005) 'Introduzione', in C. E. Gadda, *I Littoriali del Lavoro, e altri scritti giornalistici 1932–1941*, Pisa: Edizioni ETS, pp. 7–39.

Bertone, Manuela (2009) 'Gadda in guerra: strategie dell'auto-rappresentazione', *Chroniques italiennes*, web 15, 1.

Bertone, Manuela and Dombroski, Robert S. (eds) (1997) *Carlo Emilio Gadda. Contemporary Perspectives*, Toronto: Toronto University Press.

Bertoni, Federico (2001) *La verità sospetta. Gadda e l'invenzione della realtà*, Turin: Einaudi; part Chapter 2 also in *EJGS* 1/2001.

Bertoni, Federico (2011) 'Life's but a walking shadow. L'ombra del tragico nella *Cognizione del dolore*', in Pedriali (2011a).

Biondi, Benedetta (2002) 'Amleto in Gadda', *EJGS* Regular Issue 2, *EJGS* 2/2002.

Bologna, Corrado (1998) 'Il filo della storia. Tessitura della trama e ritmica del tempo narrativo fra Manzoni e Gadda', *Critica del testo*, 1, 1: 345–406; also in *EJGS* Archives.

Bonifacino, Giuseppe (2002) *Il groviglio delle parvenze. Studio su Carlo Emilio Gadda*, Bari: Palomar; part Chapter 2 also in *EJGS* Archives.

Bonifacino, Giuseppe (2007) 'Verso il mondo capovolto. Gadda migrante dall'Argentina al Maradagàl', *EJGS* Regular Issue 5, *EJGS* 5/2007.

Bonifacino, Giuseppe (2011) 'Sinfonia del destino. Guerra e verità in Gadda, "reduce senza endecasillabi"', in Pedriali (2011a).

Bouchard, Norma (2000) *Céline, Gadda, Beckett. Experimental Writings of the 1930s*, Gainesville, FL: Florida University Press.

Bouchard, Norma (2011) 'Reading Gadda from Argentina. The Case of Enrique Butti's *Indí*, or *Pasticciaccio argentino. Il romanzo medianico degli anni dimenticati di Gadda in Argentina*', in Pedriali (2011a).

Brecht, Bertolt (2004) 'On the popularity of the crime novel', *Irish Review*, 31, Irish Futures: 90–5.

Brower, Reuben A. et al. (1959) *On Translation*, Cambridge, MA: Harvard University Press.

Butor, Michel (1963) 'La sua tragica incompiutezza', *Gadda europeo*, *L'Europa letteraria*, Special Issue 4, 20–1: 52–5.

Butti, Enrique M. (1993) *Indí*, Buenos Aires: Editorial Losada; then (1994) as *Pasticciaccio argentino*, trans. by A. Morino, Milan: il Saggiatore.

Camps, Assumpta (2002) 'Per uno studio critico della fortuna di Gadda in Spagna', *EJGS* Regular Issue 2, *EJGS* 2/2002.

Carmina, Claudia (2007) *L'epistolografo bugiardo. Carlo Emilio Gadda*, Rome: Bonanno.

Carmina, Claudia (2008) 'Lo statuto diaristico del *Giornale di guerra e di prigionia di Gadda*', in A. Dolfi, N. Turi and R. Sacchettini (eds), *Memorie, autobiografie e diari nella letteratura italiana dell'Ottocento e del Novecento*, Pisa: Edizioni ETS, pp. 403–9.

Carta, Elisabetta (2010) *Cicatrici della memoria. Identità e corpo nella letteratura della grande guerra: Carlo Emilio Gadda e Blaise Cendrars*, Pisa: Edizioni ETS.

Casini, Simone (2004) 'La *Meditazione milanese* e il modello dell'ingegneria', in Savettieri et al. (2004: 31–41).

Cattaneo, Giulio [1973] (1991) *Il gran lombardo*, Turin: Einaudi; extract also in *EJGS* Archives.

Cenati, Giuliano (2010) *Disegni, bizze e fulmini. I racconti di Carlo Emilio Gadda*, Pisa: Edizioni ETS.

Cenati, Giuliano (2011) 'La guerra del Gaddus. Il *Giornale di guerra e di prigionia* di Carlo Emilio Gadda', *EJGS* Regular Issue 7, *EJGS* 7/2011.

Clerico, Giovanni (1993) 'Le détail et l'ensemble: Gadda et la traduction', in Manzotti (1993: 125–66); also in Archivio Manzotti, *EJGS* Supplement 5, *EJGS* 5/2007.

Colli, Barbara (2010) 'Il Fondo Gadda nell'Archivio Pietro Citati della Biblioteca Trivulziana', *Qdi*, n.s., 1: 227–58.

Contini, Gianfranco (1934) 'Carlo Emilio Gadda o del *pastiche*', *Solaria* (January/February); then (1989) as 'Primo approccio al *Castello di Udine*', in *Quarant'anni d'amicizia. Scritti su Carlo Emilio Gadda (1934–1988)*, Turin: Einaudi, pp. 3–10; also in *EJGS* Archives.

Cortellessa, Andrea (1998a) 'La guerra-tragedia, la guerra-lutto', in *Le notti chiare erano tutte un'alba. Antologia dei poeti italiani nella Prima guerra mondiale*, Milan: Mondadori, pp. 383–90, 421–4.

Cortellessa, Andrea (1998b) 'Gaddismo mediato. Funzioni Gadda negli ultimi dieci anni di narrativa italiana', *Allegoria*, 10, 28: 41–78.

Cortellessa, Andrea (2001) 'L'ingegnere va all'estero. Oltremontane fortune di C. E. Gadda (1987–2000)', *Qdi*, 1: 117–53.

Cortellessa, Andrea (2002) 'Il *Pasticciaccio* come teatro. Note a séguito dello spettacolo di Luca Ronconi', in G. Patrizi (ed.), *Sylvia. Studi in onore di Nino Borsellino*, Vol. II, Rome: Bulzoni, pp. 779–804.

Daniele, Antonio (2009) *La guerra di Gadda*, Udine: Gaspari.

D'Antoni, Claudio (2008) 'Il romanzo che diventa teatro all'Argentina di Roma: *Quer pasticciaccio brutto de via Merulana*', *Otto/Novecento*, n.s., 3: 35–52.

de Jorio Frisari, Giulio (1996) *Carlo Emilio Gadda filosofo milanese*, Bari: Palomar.

Deleuze, Gilles (1988) *Le pli. Leibniz et le Baroque*, Paris: Les Éditions de Minuit.

Deleuze, Gilles (2003) *Francis Bacon: The Logic of Sensation*, London and New York: Continuum.

Deleuze, Gilles and Guattari, Félix (1987) *A Thousand Plateaus: Capitalism and Schizophrenia*, London and New York: Continuum.

de Lucca, Robert (1999) 'That Awful Mess. A New Translation', *Differentia*, 8–9 (Spring-Autumn): 7–30.

de Lucca, Robert (2002) 'A translator's view of Gadda's language: the *Pasticciaccio*', *Quaderni d'Italianistica*, 23, 1: 133–61.

De Michelis, Ida (2010) *Tra il 'quid' e il 'quod'. Metamorfosi narrative di Carlo Emilio Gadda*, Pisa: Edizioni ETS.

Di Martino, Loredana (2007) 'Modernism/postmodernism. Rethinking the canon through Gadda', *EJGS* Regular Issue 5, *EJGS* 5/2007.

Dombroski, Robert S. (1970) 'The meaning of Gadda's *War Diary*', *Italica*, 47, 4: 373–86.

Dombroski, Robert S. (1984) 'Gadda: fascismo e psicanalisi', in *L'esistenza ubbidiente. Letterati italiani sotto il fascismo*, Naples: Guida, pp. 91–114; then (1999) as 'Gadda and fascism', in Dombroski (1999: 117–34); also in *EJGS* Archives.

Dombroski, Robert S. (1996) 'Gadda', in P. Brand and L. Pertile (eds), *The Cambridge History of Italian Literature*, Cambridge: Cambridge University Press, pp. 527–30.

Dombroski, Robert S. (1999) *Creative Entanglements. Gadda and the Baroque*, Toronto: Toronto University Press; then (2002) as *Gadda e il barocco*, trans. by A. R. Dicuonzo, Turin: Bollati Boringhieri, Chapter 1, 'Un'etica barocca'; also in *EJGS* 0/2000.

Dombroski, Robert S. (2003) 'The foundations of Italian modernism: Pirandello, Svevo, Gadda', in P. Bondanella and A. Ciccarelli (eds), *The Cambridge Companion to the Italian Novel*, Cambridge: Cambridge University Press, pp. 89–103.

Donnarumma, Raffaele (2001) *Gadda. Romanzo e 'pastiche'*, Palermo: Palumbo; part Chapter 4 in *EJGS* 2/2002.

Donnarumma, Raffaele (2002) 'Fascismo', in Pedriali (2008).

Donnarumma, Raffaele (ed.) (2003) *Antinomie gaddiane*, *EJGS* Supplement *n* + 1, *EJGS* 3/2003.

Donnarumma, Raffaele (2004) 'Funzione Gadda: storia di un equivoco', in Savettieri et al. (2004: 137–57).

Donnarumma, Raffaele (2006) *Gadda modernista*, Pisa: Edizioni ETS.

Empson, William (1966) *Seven Types of Ambiguity*, New York: New Directions.

Fracassa, Ugo (2011) 'Immagini, quadri, inquadrature. Cinegenicità e *adapto-génie* del *Pasticciaccio*', *EJGS* Regular Issue 7, *EJGS* 7/2011.

Frasca, Gabriele (2011) *Un quanto di erotia. Gadda con Freud e Schrödinger*, Naples: Edizioni d'if.

Freud, Sigmund [1920] (1955) 'Memorandum on the electrical treatment of war neurotics', in *The Standard Edition of the Complete Psychological Works of Sigmund Freud*, Vol. 17 (1917–19), *An Infantile Neurosis and Other Works*, edited by J. Strachey, London: Hogarth Press and the Institute of Psychoanalysis.

Fusco, Mario (1963) 'L'oeuvre de Carlo-Emilio Gadda', *Critique*, 19, 188: 21–32.

Genette, Gérard (1997) *Paratexts. Thresholds of Interpretations*, Cambridge: Cambridge University Press.

Genna, Giuseppe (2012) *Antibiologia di una nazione. La tragedia nella scena assoluta di Fabrizio Gifuni*, in Gifuni and Bertolucci (2012: 16–26).

Gersbach, Markus (1969) *Carlo Emilio Gadda – Wirklichkeit und Verzerrung*, Bern: Francke.

Gifuni, Fabrizio (2012) '*Quer pasticciaccio brutto de via Merulana*' – *letto da Fabrizio Gifuni*, Rome: Emons audiolibri.

Gifuni, Fabrizio and Bertolucci, Giuseppe (2012) *Gadda e Pasolini: antibiografia di una nazione*, Rome: Minimum Fax.

Gioanola, Elio (2004) *Carlo Emilio Gadda. Topazi e altre gioie familiari*, Milan: Jaca Book, Chapters 23–4; also in *EJGS* Archives.

Girard, René (1966) *Deceit, Desire and the Novel*, Baltimore, MD: Johns Hopkins Press.

Godioli, Alberto (2011) '*La scemenza del mondo*'. *Riso e romanzo nel primo Gadda*, Pisa: Edizioni ETS.

Grignani, Maria Antonietta (1998) 'L'Argentina di Gadda fra biografia e straniamento', *Il confronto letterario*, Quaderni del Dipartimento di Lingue e Letterature Straniere Moderne dell'Università di Pavia, 15, 29: 57–73; also in *EJGS* 0/2000.

Guglielmi, Guido (1997) 'Gadda and the form of the novel', in Bertone and Dombroski (1997: 25–42); also in *EJGS* 0/2000.

Gutkowski, Emanuela (2002) 'Un esempio di traduzione intersemiotica: dal *Pasticciaccio* a *Un maledetto imbroglio*', *EJGS* Regular Issue 2, *EJGS* 2/2002.

Hainsworth, Peter (1997) 'Fascism and anti-fascism in Gadda', in Bertone and Dombroski (1997: 221–41); then (2003) as *Gadda fascista*, trans. by R. Donnarumma, in Donnarumma (2003).

Isella, Dante (1994) *L'idillio di Meulan. Da Manzoni a Sereni*, Turin: Einaudi.

Italia, Paola (1996) 'La parodia e il simbolo. La tradizione letteraria nell'*Adalgisa* di C. E. Gadda', *Studi novecenteschi*, 23, 51: 7–46.

Italia, Paola (1998) *Glossario di Carlo Emilio Gadda 'milanese'. Da 'La meccanica' a 'L'Adalgisa'*, Alessandria: Edizioni dell'Orso; selected lemmas also in *EJGS* Glossary.

Italia, Paola (2004) 'Dal cuófeno dell'Ingegnere: lo stato delle carte', in Manzotti and Pedriali (2004).

Italia, Paola (ed.) (2007) *Editing Gadda*, *EJGS* Supplement 6, *EJGS* 6/2007.

Italia, Paola and Pinotti, Giorgio (2008) 'Edizioni d'autore coatte: il caso di *Eros e Priapo* (con l'originario primo capitolo, 1944–46)', *Ecdotica*, 5: 7–102.

Kleinhans, Martha (2005) *'Satura' und 'pasticcio'. Formen und Funktionen der Bildlichkeit im Werk Carlo Emilio Gaddas*, Tübingen: Max Niemeyer Verlag.

Lefevere, André (1992) *Translation, Rewriting and the Manipulation of Literary Fame*, London: Routledge.

Leucadi, Giancarlo (2000) *Il naso e l'anima. Saggio su C. E. Gadda*, Bologna: il Mulino; extract also in *EJGS* Regular Issue 1, *EJGS* 1/2001.

Longhi, Claudio (ed.) (1996) *Quer pasticciaccio brutto de via Merulana*, programme notes of the show directed by Luca Ronconi, 2 vols, Rome: Teatro di Roma; Part 1 also in *EJGS* Resources.

Longhi, Claudio (2001a) 'La regìa tra commento e interpretazione. *Cahier d'études* sulla storia dell'edizione teatrale di *Quer pasticciaccio* curata da Luca Ronconi', in Andreini and Tessari (2001: 99–190).

Longhi, Claudio (2001b) 'Teatrografia gaddiana', in Andreini and Tessari (2001: 299–306).

Lucchini, Guido (1987) 'Gadda lettore di Freud', *Paragone*, 448: 59–76; then (1997) as *Gadda's Freud*, in Bertone and Dombroski (1997: 177–94).

Lucchini, Guido (1994) 'Gli studi filosofici di C. E. Gadda (1924–1929)', in *Per Carlo Emilio Gadda*, Atti del Convegno di Studi, Pavia, 22–23 November 1993, *Strumenti critici*, 9, 2 (75): 223–45; also in *EJGS* Archives.

Lugnani, Lucio (2004) 'Pezzi di bravura e discorsività narrativa (sul VI tratto della *Cognizione*)', in Savettieri et al. (2004: 43–66).

McConnell, Joann (1973) *A Vocabulary Analysis of Gadda's 'Quer pasticciaccio'*, Columbia, MO: University of Missouri, Romance Monographs.

Manzotti, Emilio (ed.) (1993) *Le ragioni del dolore, Carlo Emilio Gadda 1893–1993*, Lugano: Edizioni Cenobio; also in Archivio Manzotti, *EJGS* Supplement 5, *EJGS* 5/2007.

Manzotti, Emilio (1997) 'Description by alternatives and description with comment: some characteristic procedures of Gadda's writing', in Bertone and Dombroski (1997: 61–95); also in *EJGS* 0/2000; Italian version in Archivio Manzotti, *EJGS* Supplement 5, *EJGS* 5/2007.

Manzotti, Emilio (1999) 'Carlo Emilio Gadda', in E. Malato (ed.), *Storia della letteratura italiana, Il Novecento*, Vol. IX, Rome: Salerno Editrice, pp. 605–81; original, unabridged version also in Archivio Manzotti, *EJGS* Supplement 5, *EJGS* 5/2007.

Manzotti, Emilio and Federica G., Pedriali (eds) (2004) *Disharmony Established. Festschrift for Gian Carlo Roscioni*, Proceedings of the first *EJGS* international conference, Edinburgh, 10–11 April 2003, *EJGS* Supplement 3, *EJGS* 4/2004.

Marchesini, Manuela (2007) 'Il segreto macchinismo dietro il quadrante dell'orologio. For a New Visual Rendition of Gadda's *Pasticciaccio*', *EJGS* Regular Issue 5, *EJGS* 5/2007.

Matt, Luigi (2004) 'Invenzioni lessicali gaddiane. Glossarietto di *Eros e Priapo*', *Qdi*, 3: 97–182.

Mileschi, Christophe (2007) *Gadda contre Gadda. L'écriture comme champ de bataille*, Grenoble: ELLUG, Université Stendhal.

Milton, John and Bandia, Paul (eds) (2009) *Agents of Translation*, Amsterdam: John Benjamins Publishing.

Minazzi, Fabio (2006) 'Sull'abbozzo di una (non ordinaria) tesi di laurea', *Qdi*, 4: 219–45.

Morin, Edgar (1990) *Introduction à la pensée complexe*, Paris: Seuil.

Musa, Mark (1984) 'Translator's note: on being a good lover', in Dante Alighieri, *The Divine Comedy*, Vol. 1, *Inferno*, New York: Penguin Classics, pp. 57–64.

Nancy, Jean-Luc (2000) *Being Singular Plural*, Stanford, CA: Stanford University Press.

Nord, Christiane (1997) *Translating as a Purposeful Activity: Functionalist Approaches Explained*, Manchester: St Jerome Publishing.

Papponetti, Giuseppe (2002) *Gadda – D'Annunzio e il lavoro italiano*, Rome: Fondazione Ignazio Silone.

Pecoraro, Aldo (1996) *Gadda e Manzoni, Il giallo della 'Cognizione del dolore'*, Pisa: Edizioni ETS; Chapter 1 also in *EJGS* Archives.

Pecoraro, Aldo (1998) *Gadda*, Rome and Bari: Laterza.

Pedriali, Federica G. (1999) 'Il *Pasticciaccio* e il suo doppio', *Delitti di carta*, 5: 77–86; also *EJGS* 0/2000 and, with further additions, Pedriali (2007a: 19–35).

Pedriali, Federica G. (ed.) (2003) *Eros o Logos? Il lungo sabato di Gadda*, *EJGS* Supplement 2, *EJGS* 3/2003.

Pedriali, Federica G. (2004) 'Doppifondi di romanzo. Ancora sul *Pasticciaccio* (passando per *Notte di luna*)', *EJGS* Regular Issue 4, *EJGS* 4/2004; also in Pedriali (2007a: 37–50).

Pedriali, Federica G. (2007a) *Altre carceri d'invenzione. Studi gaddiani*, Ravenna: Longo.

Pedriali, Federica G. (2007b) *Cain and Other Symmetries (the Early Alternatives)*, *EJGS* Monographs 3, *EJGS* 6/2007.

Pedriali, Federica G. (ed.) [2002, 2004] (2008) *A Pocket Gadda Encyclopedia*, *EJGS* Supplement 1, *EJGS* 2/2002, *EJGS* 4/2004.

Pedriali, Federica G. (ed.) (2011a) *Come non lavoriamo*, *EJGS* Decennial Special Supplement, *EJGS* Supplement 9, *EJGS* 7/2011.

Pedriali, Federica (G.) (2011b) 'The universe stinks (Gadda perfects our plot)', in Pedriali (2011a).

Pinotti, Giorgio (2007) 'Sul testo di *Eros e Priapo*', in Italia (2007).

Pinotti, Giorgio (2009) '"Y s'sont canardés rue Merulana, au 219", ovvero: le emigrazioni di don Ciccio Ingravallo', in *Copy in Italy. Autori italiani nel mondo dal 1945 a oggi*, edited by Fondazione Mondadori, Milan: Effigie, pp. 113–19.

Ponticelli, Paola (2003) 'Giustizia ingiusta: alcuni casi di citazioni manzoniane nel *Pasticciaccio*', *EJGS* Regular Issue 3, *EJGS* 3/2003.

Ponticelli, Paola (2004) 'La mirabile sintassi dell'ingegnere. Enumeration in Carlo Emilio Gadda', *Arachnofiles, Journal of European Languages and Cultures*, University of Edinburgh, Issue 3, Proceedings of the Postgraduate Colloquium of the Society for Italian Studies, Edinburgh, 24 May 2003.

Porro, Mario (2009) *Letteratura come filosofia naturale*, Milan: Medusa.

Porro, Mario (2011) 'Accenni eraclitei nell'ontologia di Gadda', in Pedriali (2011a).

Pucci, Piero (1967) 'The obscure sickness', *Italian Quarterly*, 11, 42: 43–62.

Riatsch, Clà (1995) 'Autoglossa e autotraduzione', in Terzoli (1995: 307–34).

Rinaldi, Rinaldo (2001) *L'indescrivibile arsenale. Ricerche intorno alle fonti della 'Cognizione del dolore'*, Milan: UNICOPLI; part Chapter 3 also in *EJGS* 2/2002.

Riva, Massimo (2002) 'Iper-romanzo', in Pedriali (2008).

Roscioni, Gian Carlo [1969, 1975] (1995a) *La disarmonia prestabilita. Studi su Gadda*, Turin: Einaudi; Chapter 1 also in *EJGS* Archives; also (1993) as *La disharmonie préétablie, Essai sur Gadda*, Paris: Seuil.

Roscioni, Gian Carlo (1995b) *Terre emerse: il problema degli indici di Gadda*, in Terzoli (1995: 23–43).

Roscioni, Gian Carlo (1997) *Il duca di Sant'Aquila. Infanzia e giovinezza di Gadda*, Milan: Mondadori; Chapter 4 also in *EJGS* Archives.

Santi, Mara (2008) 'Cinema', in Pedriali (2008).

Santovetti, Olivia (2007) 'Ramified plots: Carlo Emilio Gadda's *Quer pasticciaccio brutto de via Merulana*', in *Digression. A Narrative Strategy in the Italian Novel*, Bern: Peter Lang, pp. 133–85.

Sarina, Andrea (2001) *L'incendio di via Keplero. 'Studio 128' e 'racconto inedito' di Carlo Emilio Gadda. Con edizione commentata del testo*, *EJGS* Monographs 1, *EJGS* 1/2001.

Savettieri, Cristina (2008) *La trama continua. Storia e forme del romanzo di Gadda*, Pisa: Edizioni ETS.

Savettieri, Cristina (2009) 'Il Ventennio di Gadda', in R. Luperini and P. Cataldi (eds), *Scrittori italiani tra fascismo e antifascismo*, Pisa: Pacini, pp. 1–33.

Savettieri, Cristina, Benedetti, Carla and Lugnani, Lucio (eds) (2004) *Gadda. Meditazione e racconto*, Pisa: Edizioni ETS.

Sbragia, Albert (1996a) *Carlo Emilio Gadda and the Modern Macaronic*, Gainesville, FL: Florida University Press; introduction also in *EJGS* 0/2000.

Sbragia, Albert (1996b) 'Fear of the periphery: colonialism, class, and the South American outback in Carlo Emilio Gadda', *Modern Language Notes*, 111, 1: 38–57.

Scapinelli, Giovanna (2002) 'Il giovane Gadda attraverso il suo epistolario', *Forum Italicum*, 36, 2: 253–82.

Scarpa, Tiziano (2007) *Comuni mortali: Gli straccioni. Il professor Manganelli e l'ingegner Gadda*, Milan: Effigie.

Segre, Cesare (1985) 'Punto di vista, polifonia ed espressività nel romanzo italiano (1940–1970)', in *L'espressivismo linguistico nella letteratura italiana*, Atti dei Convegni Lincei 71, Roma, 16–18 gennaio 1984, pp. 181–94; then (1991) in *Intrecci di voci. La polifonia nella letteratura del Novecento*, Turin: Einaudi, pp. 27–44.

Segre, Cesare (2001) 'Le tre rivoluzioni di C. E. Gadda', in *Ritorno alla critica*, Turin: Einaudi, pp. 67–80.

Spiegelman, Willard (2002) 'William Weaver, the art of translation no. 3', *Paris Review*, Issue 161, http://www.theparisreview.org/interviews/421/the-art-of-translation-no-3-william-weaver (last accessed 30 June 2012).

Spila, Cristiano (2011) *Il banchetto di Gonzalo*, in Pedriali (2011a).

Stellardi, Giuseppe (1995) 'La prova dell'altro: Gadda tradotto', in Terzoli (1995: 343–62); also in *EJGS* Archives.

Stellardi, Giuseppe (2003) 'Gadda antifascista', in Donnarumma (2003).

Stellardi, Giuseppe (2006) *Gadda: miseria e grandezza della letteratura*, Florence: Franco Cesati.

Stracuzzi, Riccardo (2001) 'Retorica del racconto nel *Pasticciaccio*', *EJGS* Regular Issue 1, *EJGS* 1/2001.

Stracuzzi, Riccardo (2002) '*Pastiche*', in Pedriali (2008).

Stracuzzi, Riccardo (2007a) 'Gadda: propaganda e ironia (in margine a una recente riedizione di scritti divulgativi)', *EJGS* Regular Issue 6, *EJGS* 6/2007.

Stracuzzi, Riccardo (2007b) 'Chiose all'edizione della tesi su Leibniz', in Italia (2007).

Stracuzzi, Riccardo (ed.) (2007c) *Gadda al vaglio della critica (1931–1943)*, *EJGS* Supplement 7, *EJGS* 6/2007.

Tahir-Gürçağlar, Şenhaz (2002) 'What texts don't tell: the uses of paratexts in translation research', in T. Hermans (ed.), *Crosscultural Transgressions: Research Models in Translation Studies*, Vol. II, *Historical and Ideological Issues*, Manchester: St Jerome Publishing, pp. 44–60.

Terzoli, Maria Antonietta (ed.) (1995) *Le lingue di Gadda*, Atti del Convegno di Basilea, 10–12 dicembre 1993, Rome: Salerno Editrice.

Terzoli, Maria Antonietta (2001) 'L'anima si governa per alfabeti. Note su Gadda scrittore di guerra', in M. Rech (ed.), *La Grande Guerra: Storia e Memoria / Erster Weltkrieg: Geschichte und Erinnerung. Seminario: Letterati al fronte: i casi Gadda e Comisso*, Feltre, 14 settembre 2001, Rasai di Seren del Grappa; revised version in *EJGS* Regular Issue 3, *EJGS* 3/2003, and also Terzoli (2009: 15–31).

Terzoli, Maria Antonietta (2009) *Alle sponde del tempo consunto. Carlo Emilio Gadda dalle poesie di guerra al 'Pasticciaccio'*, Milan: Effigie.

Turolo, Antonio (1995) *Teoria e prassi linguistica nel primo Gadda*, Pisa: Giardini.

Ungarelli, Giulio (ed.) (1993a) *Gadda al microfono. L'ingegnere e la RAI 1950–1955*, Turin: Nuova ERI.

Ungarelli Giulio (1993b) 'I lettori di Gadda', in G. Sebastiani (ed.), *Catalogo delle edizioni di Carlo Emilio Gadda. Con un saggio di Giulio Ungarelli*, Milan: All'insegna del pesce d'oro.

Venuti, Lawrence (1995) *The Translator's Invisibility*, London: Routledge.

Watts, Richard (2000) 'Translating culture: reading the paratexts to Aimé Césaire's *Cahier d'un retour au pays natal*', *TTR: Traduction, Terminologie, Rédaction*, 13, 2: 29–45.

Weaver, William (1989) 'The process of translation', in J. Biguenet and R. Schulte (eds), *The Craft of Translation*, Chicago: Chicago University Press, pp. 117–24; also in *EJGS* BabelGadda.

Weaver, William (ed.) (1999) *Open City. Seven Writers in Postwar Rome*, South Royalton, VT: Steerforth Press.

Wehling-Giorgi, Katrin (2011) 'Defilement, war and the corpse: on abjection in Carlo Emilio Gadda's and Louis-Ferdinand Céline's writings', *EJGS* Regular Issue 7, *EJGS* 7/2011.

Wieser, Dagmar (1995) 'D'un fraterno lutto (Appunti per una lettura freudiana di Gadda)', in Terzoli (1995: 81–148).

Zancanella, Silvia (1995) *La parola in bilico. La scrittura intima nel Novecento e la produzione epistolare di Carlo Emilio Gadda*, Venice: il Cardo.

Zollino, Antonio (1998) *Il vate e l'ingegnere. D'Annunzio in Gadda*, Pisa: Edizioni ETS; Chapter 2 also in *EJGS* Archives.

Zublena, Paolo (2002) 'La scienza del dolore. Il linguaggio tecnico scientifico nel Gadda narratore', in *L'inquietante simmetria della lingua. Il linguaggio tecnico-scientifico nella narrativa italiana del Novecento*, Alessandria: Edizioni dell'Orso, pp. 33–63; also in *EJGS* Archives.

Contributors

Giuseppe Episcopo (PhD Candidate Italian Studies, University of Edinburgh) has a PhD in Modern Philology (University of Naples Federico II) and was visiting scholar at Columbia University. He edited and translated Fredric Jameson's *Brecht and Method* (Cronopio, 2008) and has published on Stefano D'Arrigo, Carlo Emilio Gadda, William Goyen, Thomas Pynchon, Arno Schmidt, Federigo Tozzi and J. Rodolfo Wilcock in books and journals. His monograph on Thomas Pynchon and Stefano D'Arrigo *L'eredità della fine* is forthcoming (:duepunti, 2013).

Christopher John Ferguson has both his undergraduate and PhD degrees from the University of Edinburgh. He has mainly worked on Carlo Emilio Gadda and his doctoral thesis was on Gadda's use of the religious and the scientific. Christopher is also interested in detective fiction and twentieth-century literature. He is the translator of *Giustina* by Lilia Amadio.

Fabrizio Gifuni is one of Italy's leading actors. His career successfully combines cinema and theatre. He has worked with Gianni Amelio, Marco Tullio Giordana, Giuseppe Bertolucci, Liliana Cavani, Antonio Capuano and Ridley Scott, and has created and interpreted several works for stage performance. With Giuseppe Bertolucci, between 2002 and 2012 he developed a project on Gadda and Pasolini which resulted in two plays, *'Na specie de cadavere lunghissimo* and *L'ingegner Gadda va alla guerra o della tragica istoria di Amleto Pirobutirro* (2010 Ubu Prize for both Best Actor and Best Show of the year), now also presented as *Gadda e Pasolini, antibiografia di una nazione* (Minimum Fax, 2012). His audio-book *'Quer pasticciaccio brutto de via Merulana'* – *letto da Fabrizio Gifuni* has just been released (Emons, 2012). Recent awards for his outstanding career in the arts include the Federico Fellini Prize (2011) and the Gianmaria Volonté Award (2012).

ALBERTO GODIOLI (PhD Scuola Normale Superiore, Pisa, 2012) has worked on the Italian short story between the two World Wars, focusing on its comic and humoristic inflections. He was Visiting Gadda Fellow at the University of Edinburgh (2011) and is Senior Editorial Assistant of the *Edinburgh Journal of Gadda Studies*. His publications include the monograph *'La scemenza del mondo'. Riso e romanzo nel primo Gadda* (ETS, 2011; winner Gadda First 2012, early career category of the Edinburgh Gadda Prize), as well as articles on Sanguineti, Bassani, Campana, Pascoli and Ariosto. Alberto is embarking on a grammar of laughter in the realist novel from Balzac to Gadda as part of his Newton International Fellowship at the University of Edinburgh (2013–14).

CRISTINA OLIVARI studied Foreign European Languages at Ca' Foscari University, Venice, where she graduated with a dissertation on the English translation of *Quer pasticciaccio brutto de via Merulana*. She later earned an MSc in Theory and Practice of Translation at the University of Edinburgh. Her final dissertation further developed her previous studies on Gadda's Roman detective novel. Cristina is completing her PhD at the same university. Her research applies translation theory to Gadda's circulation in English and French.

FEDERICA G. PEDRIALI is Professor of Literary Metatheory and Modern Italian Studies and Head of Italian at the University of Edinburgh. She is the Director of the Edinburgh Gadda Projects, Director and General Editor of the *Edinburgh Journal of Gadda Studies*, Chair of the Edinburgh Gadda Prize, Chair of the Nicola Benedetti Scholarship Fund and Director of the ISRC Italo-Scottish Research Centre funded by the Carnegie Trust for the Universities of Scotland. Federica has published extensively on the contemporary canon. Her books include *La farmacia degli incurabili. Da Collodi a Calvino* (Longo, 2006 – winner Nuove Lettere 2005; runner-up Mario Soldati 2006) and *Altre carceri d'invenzione. Studi gaddiani* (Longo, 2007). She is currently working on a two-volume project *The Universe Stinks. Props, Gaps and Last Subjects, From Bruno to Gadda* (vol. 1) and *From Freud to Foucault* (vol. 2), editing the print edition of the *Pocket Gadda Encyclopedia* (4 vols, 2013) and co-editing the first volume of the new ISRC Series on the Italian Diaspora, *No-Where-Next | War-Diaspora-Origin* (2013).

Index

Adalgisa – Disegni milanesi, L', 44, 56, 143
  Adalgisa, 67
Adamo, Sergia, 71
Adelphi Edizioni, 17, 66, 72, 128
Adorno, Theodor W., 136
Agosti, Stefano, 68
Alighieri, Dante, 34, 59, 145
Amigoni, Ferdinando, 68
'Amleto' al Teatro Valle, 127, 148
Andreini, Alba, 71, 72
Antonello, Pierpaolo, 36, 63, 70
Appiah, Kwame Anthony, 19
Arbasino, Alberto, 66, 67, 72

Baccelli, Monique, 28
Bacon, Francis, 40
Baldi, Valentino, 64, 71
Balzac, Honoré de, 7, 71
Bandia, Paul, 18
baroque, 7, 9, 38, 51, 60, 62, 70, 135
Bateson, Gregory, 63
Battisti, Cesare, 98, 99
Beckett, Samuel, 7, 60
Bellow, Saul, 10
Benedetti, Carla, 37, 63, 64, 70, 71
Benjamin, Walter, 38
Bernini, Marco, 70

Berto, Giuseppe, 13
Bertolucci, Giuseppe, 44
Bertone, Manuela, 60, 68
Bertoni, Federico, 63, 68, 70
Bologna, Corrado, 71
Bonifacino, Giuseppe, 39, 63, 68, 70
Borges, Jorge Luis, 10
Bouchard, Norma, 60, 66, 68
Braziller, George, 11, 12, 13, 14
Brecht, Bertold, 42
Brower, Reuben, 34
Bruno, Giordano, 7, 59
Butor, Michel, 10

Caesar, Julius, 124, 125, 130
Calvino, Italo, 8
Campanella, Tommaso, 133
Camps, Assumpta, 71
Capgras, Joseph, 124, 125
Caporetto, 38, 102, 103, 106, 107, 129, 137
Cardinale, Claudia, 12
Carmina, Claudia, 68
Carta, Elisabetta, 39, 68
Carutti, Giuseppina, 45
Casini, Simone, 70
Castello di Udine, Il, 64, 69
Cattaneo, Giulio, 67
Céline, Ferdinand, 7, 60, 71

Cenati, Giuliano, 39, 68, 71
Cervantes, Miguel de, 7
Clerico, Giovanni, 71
Cognizione del dolore, La, 9, 10, 12,
    13, 14, 21, 58, 64, 68, 70, 127,
    143
  Acquainted with Grief, 9, 12, 13,
    137
Colli, Barbara, 73
Come lavoro, 37, 144
Conrad, Joseph, 7
Contini, Gianfranco, 7, 59, 69
Cortellessa, Andrea, 66, 68, 71, 72

d'Annunzio, Gabriele, 71
D'Antoni, Claudio, 72
Darwin, Charles, 70, 137
de Jorio Frisari, Giulio, 63, 70
de Lucca, Robert, 14–16, 19, 71
De Michelis, Ida, 71
Deleuze, Gill, 40, 42, 62, 70
Derrida, Jacques, 136
Di Martino, Loredana, 60
Dickens, Charles, 71
Dombroski, Robert S., 38, 56, 60,
    62, 63, 68, 70, 71
Donnarumma, Raffaele, 64, 65, 66,
    70, 71, 72
Dostoevsky, Fyodor, 7, 71
Duca di Sant'Aquila (Carlo Emilio
    Gadda), 23, 67, 84, 85

Eco, Umberto, 8
*Edinburgh Journal of Gadda
    Studies, The (EJGS)*, 15, 16, 61,
    63, 66, 68
Einaudi, Giulio, 12
Empson, William, 64
Eros e Priapo, 20, 24, 25, 29, 30,
    36, 38, 41, 42, 44, 65, 66, 67,
    68, 69, 128, 129, 136, 141,
    142, 144

fascism, 2, 30, 33, 38, 41, 42, 51,
    64, 65, 68, 69, 129, 130, 136,
    141, 142, 144
father, *padre*, 90, 91, 92, 93, 94, 95,
    103, 114, 115, 116, 118, 119,
    136, 137
Fish, Stanley, 72
Flaubert, Gustave, 7
Folengo, Teofilo, 7
Frasca, Gabriele, 63, 70
Freud, Sigmund, 38, 60, 68, 70
Fulmine sul 220, Un, 58, 70
Fusco, Mario, 10

Gadda, Clara, 92, 93, 104, 105,
    106, 107
Gadda, Enrico, 40, 65, 92, 93, 94,
    95, 104, 105, 106, 107, 132
Gaddus (Carlo Emilio Gadda), 23,
    84, 85, 86, 87, 96, 97
Garzanti, Livio, 12
Genette, Gérard, 18
Genna, Giuseppe, 72
Germi, Pietro, 12, 13, 43, 72
  Un maledetto imbroglio, 12, 43,
    72
Gersbach, Markus, 10
Gifuni, Fabrizio, 2, 8, 17, 18, 19,
    20, 21, 30, 31, 32, 33, 37, 41,
    42, 44, 45, 65, 69, 72, 135, 136
Gioanola, Elio, 68
Giornale di guerra e di prigionia, 20,
    21, 23, 28, 36, 38, 39, 40, 41,
    42, 127, 129
Girard, René, 132
Gödel, Kurt, 63
Godioli, Alberto, 64, 71
Goldsmith, Oliver, 22
Gruppo 63, 13
Guattari, Félix, 42
Guglielmi, Guido, 64, 71
Gutkowski, Emanuela, 44, 72

Hainsworth, Peter, 65, 68
Heisenberg, Werner, 37
Hobbes, Thomas, 137

Incendio di via Keplero, L', 11, 44
  The fire on via Keplero, 11
Isella, Dante, 59, 66, 69, 70, 72
Isonzo, battaglia dell', 102
Italia, Paola, 66, 68, 69, 72, 73,
  128
  Wiki Gadda, 66

Jørgensen, Conni Kay, 10
Joyce, James, 7, 60, 71

Kafka, Franz, 7
Kant, Immanuel, 37
Kienlechner, Toni, 9
Kleinhans, Martha, 71

Lampedusa, Giuseppe Tomasi di,
  8
Laplace, Simon, 26
Lefevere, André, 18
Leibniz, Gottfried Wilhelm von, 37,
  51, 62, 69, 70, 142
Leucadi, Giancarlo, 68
Levi, Primo, 8
Liberati, Arnaldo, 73
  Liberati Archives, 63, 67, 72
Longhi, Claudio, 44, 72
Longone, 92, 93
Lucchini, Guido, 70

Madonna dei Filosofi, La, 19
  The Philosophers' Madonna,
  19
Manzoni, Alessandro, 71, 88, 89
Manzotti, Emilio, 63, 69, 70, 72
Marchesini, Manuela, 44
Martignoni, Clelia, 72
Mathew, Jackson, 34

Matt, Luigi, 69
Meditazione milanese, 14, 27, 36,
  54, 63, 67, 69, 70, 142, 143,
  144, 145
Melville, Antony, 19
Meraviglie d'Italia, Le, 143
Mileschi, Christophe, 39, 68
Milton, John, 18
Minazzi, Fabio, 70
Morante, Elsa, 8
More, Thomas, 133
Morin, Edgar, 62, 63, 65
mother, *madre*, 13, 65, 82, 83, 92,
  93, 94, 95, 107, 113, 127
Musa, Mark, 34
Musil, Robert, 7
Mussolini, Benito, 24, 29, 30, 41,
  130, 144
  Cacchio, 29, 112
  Cavolini, 112
  Doosh-y, 29, 30, 42, 113
  epithets (listing), 130, 144
  kuce, il Kuce, 29, 30, 112
  Moo-so-leeny, 30, 113

Nabokov, Vladimir, 7
Nancy, Jean-Luc, 136
Nord, Christiane, 33, 34, 35

Opinione sul neorealismo, Un', 41,
  130

Papponetti, Giuseppe, 71
Pasolini, Pier Paolo, 8, 72
Pecoraro, Aldo, 68, 71
Pedriali, Federica G., 16, 19, 37, 43,
  60, 63, 64, 65, 68, 71
Pinotti, Giorgio, 66, 68, 69, 71, 72,
  73, 128
Pirandello, Luigi, 8, 71, 134, 136
Pirobutirro, Amleto, 17, 39, 42, 82,
  83, 102, 103, 127

Pirobutirro, Gonzalo, 14, 134
Plato, 133, 141, 144
Porro, Mario, 63, 70
Primo libro delle Favole, Il, 58
Prix International de Littérature, 9, 10, 11, 13
Pucci, Piero, 10
Pynchon, Thomas, 7

Quaderni dell'ingegnere, I, 66
Quer pasticciaccio brutto de via Merulana, 9, 10, 11, 12, 13, 14, 15, 19, 29, 30, 43, 44, 45, 49, 59, 62, 66, 68, 71, 72
Die grässliche Bescherung in der Via Merulana, 9
That Awful Mess on Via Merulana, 9, 12, 15, 16, 50, 63, 143
Quevedo, Francisco de, 135

Racconto italiano di ignoto del novecento, 14, 70, 133
Riatsch, Clà, 71
Rinaldi, Rinaldo, 71
Riva, Massimo, 64
Ronconi, Luca, 44, 66, 72, 136
Roscioni, Gian Carlo, 12, 37, 63, 65, 66, 67, 69, 70, 137

Salandra, Antonio, 90, 91
Santi, Mara, 43
Santovetti, Olivia, 60, 71
Savettieri, Cristina, 64, 65, 69, 71
Sbragia, Albert, 60, 70, 71
Scapinelli, Giovanna, 68
Schivazzappa, Piero, 44
Segre, Cesare, 69, 70
Shakespeare, William, 21, 22, 31, 58, 134

Hamlet, 21, 32, 42, 55, 127, 128, 134
Hamlet, 1, 10, 14, 39, 40, 55, 56, 79, 81, 83, 93, 94, 95, 103, 107, 117, 134
Spiegelman, Willard, 11
Spinoza, Baruch, 37
Stellardi, Giuseppe, 68, 70, 71
Sterne, Laurence, 7
Tristram Shandy, 55
Stracuzzi, Riccardo, 65, 68, 70, 71
Svevo, Italo, 8, 66, 71
Swift, Jonathan, 7

Tabucchi, Antonio, 8
Tahir-Gürçağlar, Şenhaz, 18
Terzoli, Maria Antonietta, 65, 68
Tessari, Roberto, 72
Turolo, Antonio, 69

Ungarelli, Giulio, 43, 71

Vela, Claudio, 72
Vergil (Publius Vergilius Maro), 68, 127
Viaggi la morte, I, 144
Von Bertalanffy, Ludwig von, 63

Watts, Richard, 18
Weaver, William, 11, 12, 13, 14, 15, 19, 20, 24, 30, 32, 71
Wehling-Giorgi, Katrin, 60
Wieser, Dagmar, 68
World War I, 1, 28, 33, 38, 41, 65, 68
World War II, 11, 64

Zancanella, Silvia, 68
Zollino, Antonio, 71
Zublena, Paolo, 69